"As usual, Stephanie Sarkis has done a masterful job of assembling a countless number of tips and strategies to improve the lives of adults with ADD. Whether you're brand new to the diagnosis or an experienced old-timer, you will find plenty of useful ideas. Don't let this book's small size fool you—it's loaded with great stuff."

—Ari Tuckman, PsyD, MBA, author of
Understand Your Brain, Get More Done;
More Attention, Less Deficit; and *Integrative Treatment for Adult ADHD*

"Sarkis combines her wealth of information with the latest research findings for an enriched second edition of this popular book. The book is concise and to the point on issues that challenge adults with ADD and their families. Skills offered in this book will enhance daily productivity and self-confidence, leading to a more satisfying life. Buy the book and use what she has to offer. It can only help."

—David W. Goodman, MD, assistant professor
at Johns Hopkins School of Medicine and
director at Adult Attention Deficit Disorder
Center of Maryland

"Stephanie Sarkis has given me a terrific guide for the next phase of my life as I enter medical school. She dispels the myths about ADD and presents the latest research in a way everyone can understand."

—Blake E. S. Taylor, author of *ADHD and Me*
and medical student at Columbia University

W9-AZT-966

"Adults with ADD want and need a simple, practical plan that works to help tame the chaos in their lives, and that's exactly what Stephanie Sarkis gives them in the second edition of *10 Simple Solutions to Adult ADD*. Expanded to include the latest technology and research, Sarkis includes easy-to-follow strategies for everyday problems from remembering to take your medication to tiding up your closet. I know I'll continue to recommend this book as a must-have for all adults with ADD."

> —Patricia O. Quinn, MD, director of the
> National Center for Girls and Women with
> AD/HD

"Stephanie Sarkis shows you how to jump-start your life and plow through any obstacles in *10 Simple Solutions to Adult ADD*. These easy-to-read and easy-to-use tools will take your life to the next level. An eloquent and engaging guide to thriving with adult ADD."

> —Lara Honos-Webb, PhD, author of *The Gift of Adult ADD*

"Part roadmap and part condensed travel guide, *10 Simple Solutions to Adult ADD* hits the highlights of medication, organization, and self-care. Sarkis' to-the-point prose and realistic strategies help keep you on track."

> —Gina Pera, award-winning journalist and
> author of *Is It You, Me, or Adult ADD?*

"*10 Simple Solutions to Adult ADD* is a straightforward, honest book jam-packed with valuable tips and strategies. Stephanie Sarkis writes as if she is standing right with you, coaching you through various aspects of the ADD life. Each chapter stands alone and is filled with techniques that you can start using right now to achieve the balance that is essential for a happy, healthy life."

—Roberto Olivardia, PhD, clinical instructor in the department of psychiatry at Harvard Medical School and clinical associate in psychology at McLean Hospital

"This book is a must-have guide for people with ADD! In *10 Simple Solutions to Adult ADD*, Sarkis helps readers gain an in-depth understanding of the way their ADD affects various areas of their life. She offers simple practical exercises, current information, and helpful resources to enable readers to move forward to improve their lives. What really makes this book powerful are all of the ADD-friendly strategies that are key to helping make things stick!"

—Nancy A. Ratey, EdM, MCC, SCAC, strategic life coach and author of *The Disorganized Mind*

10

Simple Solutions
to Adult ADD

SECOND EDITION

How to Overcome
Chronic Distraction &
Accomplish Your Goals

STEPHANIE MOULTON SARKIS, PhD

New Harbinger Publications, Inc.

Distributed in Canada by Raincoast Books

Copyright © 2011 by Stephanie Moulton Sarkis
New Harbinger Publications, Inc.
5674 Shattuck Avenue
Oakland, CA 94609
www.newharbinger.com

Cover design by Amy Shoup; Text design by Michele Waters-Kermes; Acquired by Melissa Kirk; Edited by Carole Honeychurch

Printed in Canada

Library of Congress Cataloging-in-Publication Data

Sarkis, Stephanie.
  10 simple solutions to adult add : how to overcome chronic distraction and accomplish your goals / Stephanie Moulton Sarkis. -- 2nd ed.
      p. cm.
  Includes bibliographical references.
  ISBN 978-1-60882-184-6 (pbk.) -- ISBN 978-1-60882-185-3 (pdf e-book) -- ISBN 978-1-60882-186-0 (epub)
  1. Attention-deficit disorder in adults--Popular works. 2. Attention-deficit disorder in adults--Treatment--Popular works. 3. Self-care, Health--Popular works. I. Title. II. Title: Ten simple solutions to adult ADD. III. Title: Ten simple solutions to adult attention-deficit disorder.
  RC394.A85S26 2011
  616.85'89--dc23

                              2011029639

15   14   13

10   9   8   7   6   5   4   3   2

This book is dedicated to all my clients and patients, whose strength I admire. They have taught me the most about ADD.

Contents

Notes on the Second Edition

Since the first edition of *10 Simple Solutions to Adult ADD* was published in 2006, there has been even more research regarding the genetic and biological roots of ADD, and there are also more medications available for the treatment of ADD. In addition, technology has changed rapidly since 2006. Smartphones have become the rule, not the exception; "paperless" living is becoming even more of a reality, and "apps" have become a new tool for helping someone stay organized. In this second edition of *10 Simple Solutions to Adult ADD*, you will learn how these changes have impacted the lives of people with ADD.

Acknowledgments

Thank you to all the readers of *10 Simple Solutions to Adult ADD*, for you have made this second edition possible. Thank you to my editors at New Harbinger, Melissa Kirk, Heather Garnos, and Jessica Beebe, for providing feedback and support. Thank you to Janice Moulton, Claude Moulton, William Moulton, Toby Sarkis, and Lucy Sarkis for their support. Thank you also to the clinicians whose research and support have made this book possible.

Introduction

Do you lose things? Do you interrupt people? Are you forgetful? While everyone experiences these problems occasionally, people with *attention deficit disorder* (ADD) experience these problems and more on a daily basis.

This book is for people who have recently been diagnosed with ADD or suspect they may have ADD. However, even if you have known for quite some time that you have ADD, this book can still provide solutions for some common frustrations. While this book does not go into great detail about the disorder, I will provide additional resources at the end of each chapter.

How to Use This Book

The strategies in this book will not make your ADD go away, but they can help make your life more manageable. When you have ADD, you can get overwhelmed by change. Pick one solution in the beginning and see if it works. If it does, great! Try another solution when you feel you have the first one well incorporated into your lifestyle.

It is okay if you can only read parts of the book at a time. When you have ADD, it can be difficult to read for an extended period of time. It is also okay to skip around the book to take bits and pieces of information that suit your needs. There is an exercise at the end of each chapter. These exercises give you an in-depth look at how ADD influences your life. They can also help you fine-tune your plan for change.

An Overview of Simple Solutions for Adult ADD

Let's begin by looking at what this book will cover. Chapter 1 gives an overview of the symptoms, myths, and facts about ADD. Chapter 2 discusses medication, a proven effective treatment for ADD. Chapter 3 provides solutions for clutter and guides you in getting organized. Chapter 4 is about developing a system that helps you avoid losing items. In chapter 5, I'll offer time management strategies that work for people with ADD. Chapter 6 discusses solutions for money management difficulties. In chapter 7, I'll discuss ways you can achieve physical, emotional, and spiritual wellness. Chapter 8 discusses which careers are best for people with ADD. Because ADD can cause certain social difficulties, developing better social skills is covered in chapter 9. Chapter 10 discusses techniques that can improve your relationships.

1

Understanding ADD

John is late for work again. He couldn't find his car keys, and then his car wouldn't start because he left the lights on last night. He has a big presentation at work, but he didn't back up his laptop and he lost the notes for his presentation when it crashed. When he walked into the building this morning, he wasn't looking where he was going and walked into someone, spilling his coffee on him. He didn't get a lot of sleep last night because he and his wife got into an argument about how she feels he does not listen to her. To top it all off, she was upset that he didn't remember to pick up some milk and eggs at the store on the way home from work last night.

Sally got embarrassed at the staff meeting again. She was thinking about what she was going to do with her day off tomorrow when the boss asked, "Sally, what are your ideas on what Bob just said?" Sally had no idea what Bob had said because she could hardly pay attention after thirty minutes of such a boring meeting. She became flustered. Why did this always seem to happen to her?

Does this sound like you?

What Is ADD?

Approximately 4.4 percent of adults in the United States have ADD, also known as *ADHD,* or *attention deficit/hyperactivity disorder* (Kessler et al. 2005). As you've probably discovered by now, ADD affects every aspect of your life: work, home, and even your social life.

What does it mean to have ADD? Symptoms include

- having mood swings

- abusing substances

- putting too many activities on your schedule

- making a lot of to-do lists and never using them

- getting lots of speeding tickets

- getting your license suspended for not paying tickets

- having feelings of not living up to your potential

- chronically procrastinating

- impulsively taking risks

- having difficulties finishing projects

- frequently losing items

- having a quick temper

- having problems with organization

- having a series of marriages

- impulsively quitting jobs

- changing jobs frequently

- lacking friends

- having difficulties managing money

- having low self-esteem

- being underemployed (working below your ability)

- disliking traffic so much that you will drive out of your way to avoid it

- interrupting people

Many adults with ADD were diagnosed with childhood ADD, but this is not always the case.

It might surprise you to learn that ADD is not all negative. There are also positive aspects to having ADD, and it is likely that you have these traits as well. People with ADD can have

- creativity

- an ability to multitask effectively

- a good sense of humor

- versatility

- the ability to let go of grudges

- a talent for thinking "outside the box"

- the drive to focus on something they are interested in

ADD can look different in different individuals. One person with ADD may have a big problem with interrupting other people, and another person's biggest ADD problem may be losing things. Also, a range of behavior can appear in a single individual. A person with ADD may not be okay in a certain situation and then be okay in the same situation later, or vice versa. For example, one very bright college student had an A, a B, a C, and a D in one semester and had all A's the next semester. Changes like this can mystify your family and friends, and even more important, they can mystify you.

The symptoms of ADD can cause a great deal of difficulty in your life. Everyone has had at least some of these symptoms at one time or another, but as a person with ADD, you live with most of these symptoms most of the time. Adult ADD can compromise your ability to do your job, get along with your family, or have stable friendships. Here are some clues that ADD is causing you difficulty:

- You have been fired from a job due to your inability to concentrate or stay organized.

- You have been reprimanded at work for not completing assignments.

- Your significant other has insisted that you get help.

- You have problems maintaining long-term friendships.

- You have been reprimanded at work for losing your temper.

- You have difficulties getting along with your family or roommates.

- You have a substance abuse problem.

- You have legal difficulties, such as arrests or multiple speeding tickets.

- Your underachieving has led to low self-esteem or depression.

- You are losing time and money due to your inability to stay organized.

- You bounce checks.

- You are in trouble with the IRS for not paying your taxes on time.

- You get late fees on your bills because you forget to pay them on time.

- You have had to file for bankruptcy due to poor money management.

- You are feeling that there is no point to your life, and you are feeling hopeless.

Myths About ADD

ADD is not really a problem with paying attention. If you have ADD, you can pay attention, especially to things that interest you. However, your brain has difficulty keeping your attention focused.

ADD affects the *frontal lobes* of the brain. The frontal lobe conducts tasks known as *executive functions*. These functions include organizing and processing information, making decisions, planning ahead, regulating moods, storing information, learning from mistakes and consequences, starting tasks, and making sure everything is working the way it should (Brown 2009; Barkley 2005). When you have ADD, you have impairment in these executive functions resulting in forgetfulness, difficulty getting motivated, an inclination to lose items, a tendency to interrupt others, *hyperfocusing* (which makes it difficult to switch tasks), and even increased mood swings.

Most people do not grow out of ADD, as is commonly believed. Approximately 50 to 67 percent of children with ADD continue to suffer from it when they are adults (Wilens 2004; Barkley et al. 2002). Your ADD behaviors may have changed since you were a child, but they can still make your life difficult. For example, when you were a child, you may have had problems with running around too much. As an adult, you may have an inner feeling of restlessness instead. As a child, you may have had difficulties waiting your turn when playing games. Now you cannot stand waiting in traffic. You may have experienced changes in your ADHD symptoms as you got older because your brain matures with age. However, as mature as it gets, your brain never really functions the same as a brain without ADD (McAlonan et al. 2009).

An explosion of research on ADD has occurred in the past few decades. ADD is a medically recognized disorder with a genetic basis and prognosis. Yes, some people may be mis-diagnosed with ADD, just as with other disorders. However, there are many more people with ADD who are undiagnosed. These missed diagnoses are important because ADD is a serious disorder that impacts all aspects of life. Adults with ADD have a significantly lower socioeconomic status, lower level of academic achievement, and higher medical costs than their non-ADD peers (Kleinman et al. 2009; Bernfort, Nordfeldt, and Persson 2008). Adults with ADD are also more likely to be unemployed. One study found that only 24 percent of ADD adults were employed, compared to 79 percent of non-ADD adults. This rate of employment improved with treatment for ADD symptoms (Halmey et al. 2009).

Adults with ADD also engage in more high-risk behaviors (such as gambling) and have a higher rate of substance abuse, more injuries, and more car accidents than non-ADD adults (Breyer et al. 2009; Sabuncuoglu 2007; Wilens and Upadhyaya 2007). They also have a higher rate of unplanned pregnan-cies and sexually transmitted diseases, compared with people without ADD (Barkley, Murphy, and Fischer 2008; Flory et al. 2006; Barkley et al. 2005).

What Causes ADD?

Why is it important to talk about the cause of ADD? If you understand that ADD is a biological disorder, you will hope-fully feel less guilt or self-blame about your ADD. Poor morals do not cause ADD. (In the 1900s, ADD was seen as a defect in moral control.) A poor diet does not cause ADD. You did not get ADD from bad parenting. Many parents blame themselves for their child's ADD. Some parents are told that if they just disciplined their child more, their child would straighten up.

ADD is highly genetic, meaning that it is passed on through the genes you inherit from your parents. If you have ADD, there is a 75 percent chance that you inherited ADD genes from at least one of your parents (Rietveld et al. 2004). Scientists have identified several genes that are associated with ADD (Guan et al. 2009). There are also hundreds of gene variations that appear to be unique to children who have ADD (Elia et al. 2010). Considering the advances in science, it is expected that more ADD-related genes and gene variations will be identified every year.

Can you think of anyone in your family who has the same problems paying attention that you do? Tracing your family history can increase your awareness of the genetic component of ADD. The exercise at the end of this chapter will help you do that.

There are other biological causes for ADD. There are brain differences in people with ADD. In children with ADD, there is a disconnect between the frontal cortex of the brain, which regulates attention, and the visual-processing areas of the brain. This difference does not occur in non-ADD children. This means that the way the brain pays attention is biologically different in those with ADD (Mazaheri et al. 2010). In addition to these brain differences, people with ADD have a low level of a neurotransmitter (or brain chemical) called *dopamine* (Volkow et al. 2009). Medications, such as stimulants, increase the level of dopamine in the brain to a normal level. I will talk more about these medications in chapter 2.

A person's environment can make ADD appear better or worse. If it was acceptable for you to move around the room during office meetings, you probably would be able to focus better. Changing your environment can help you work with your ADD. I will talk later in the book about how to make your environment more ADD friendly.

Exercise: Create Your Family Tree of ADD

1. On a large piece of paper, draw a diagram of your family tree.

2. Underneath your relatives' names, write "ADD" if you know or suspect they had ADD. Remember, the disorder was not as commonly known in years past. People may have had symptoms of ADD but were never diagnosed.

3. Also write down which family members had drug or alcohol addiction. This can be a sign of ADD since as many as one in five people with ADD has had a problem with addiction (Wilens and Upadhyaya 2007).

4. Ask your family members about any relatives you do not know a lot about.

When you are creating your family tree, think about the following questions:

- What do you notice about the pattern of ADD in your family tree?

- What do you notice about the pattern of drug and alcohol addiction in your family tree?

- Are the people with ADD and the people with addiction one and the same?

- Does anyone in your family seem eccentric? Do they do things that are outside the realm of normal behavior?

- Does anyone in your family have learning disabilities? There is a higher rate of learning disabilities among people who have ADD.

You may want to share your discoveries with others in your family. ADD can be inherited, and it is likely that some of your biological relatives had or have the disorder.

Here's an example of a family tree.

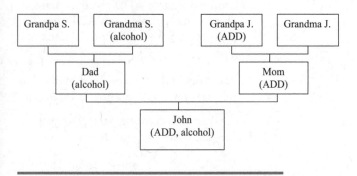

In this chapter, you learned the causes of ADD. You also learned the myths and facts about ADD. In the next chapter, you will learn about medications available for people with ADD.

Resources

Adler, L. 2007. *Scattered Minds: Hope and Help for Adults with Attention Deficit Hyperactivity Disorder*. New York: Perigee Trade.

Barkley, R.A. 2010. *Taking Charge of Adult ADHD*. New York: The Guilford Press.

Hallowell, E., and J. Ratey. 1995. *Driven to Distraction: Recognizing and Coping with Attention Deficit Disorder from Childhood Through Adulthood*. New York: Touchstone.

Hallowell, E.M., and J.J. Ratey. 2010. *Answers to Distraction*. New York: Anchor Books.

Hallowell, E.M., and J.J. Ratey. 2005. *Delivered from Distraction: Getting the Most Out of Life with Attention Deficit Disorder*. New York: Ballantine Books.

Honos-Webb, L. 2008. *The Gift of Adult ADD: How to Transform Your Challenges & Build on Your Strengths*. Oakland, CA: New Harbinger Publications, Inc.

Kelly, K., and P. Ramundo. 2006. *You Mean I'm Not Lazy, Stupid or Crazy?!: The Classic Self-Help Book for Adults with Attention Deficit Disorder*. New York: Scribner.

Sarkis, S. 2011. *Adult ADD: A Guide for the Newly Diagnosed*. Oakland, CA: New Harbinger Publications, Inc.

Tuckman, A. 2009. *More Attention, Less Deficit: Success Strategies for Adults with ADHD*. Plantation, FL: Specialty Press, Inc.

Weiss, L. 2005. Attention Deficit Disorder in Adults: A Different Way of Thinking, 4th ed. New York: Taylor Trade Publishing.

ADD Consults
www.addconsults.com

ADD Forums
www.addforums.com

A.D.D. Warehouse
www.addwarehouse.com
(800) 233-9273

ADDitude magazine
www.additudemag.com

ADDvance
www.addvance.com

Attention Deficit Disorder Association
www.add.org

Attention magazine
www.chadd.org

**Children and Adults with Attention-Deficit/
Hyperactivity Disorder**
www.chadd.org

2

Medication

In chapter 1, you learned about the symptoms and causes of ADD. In this chapter, you will learn about a proven treatment for ADD: medication. Because ADD is a biological disorder, medication remains the most effective treatment for ADD.

Medication is a foundation that will make other coping strategies more effective. As I mentioned in chapter 1, studies have shown that people with ADD have a low level of the brain chemical dopamine. When you have low dopamine, you will—without realizing it—find things that increase your dopamine level, including fidgeting, gambling, caffeine, illegal drugs, food, cigarettes, and alcohol. Medications for ADD replace or renew the neurotransmitters that your brain lacks so you feel better without needing to engage in risky behavior.

Medications do not cure your ADD, nor do they totally eliminate your symptoms. Moreover, the medications may not work right away. However, they can make at least a small difference in your functioning every day. When you add it up over a year's time, that's a huge difference.

A common misconception is that you will become addicted to medication for ADD. Most medications used to treat ADD are in a class of drugs called *stimulants*. These stimulant medications are regulated by the U.S. government and are not addictive if taken as prescribed. In fact, people who take stimulant medication for their ADD have a much lower rate of substance abuse than people who do not take medication (Mannuzza et al. 2008; Wilens et al. 2003). One of the reasons this happens is that people who take medication for their ADD have a safe way of increasing the level of dopamine and other neurotransmitters in the brain that were either missing or at low levels.

Types of Medications

The Food and Drug Administration of the United States (FDA) approves and regulates medications. The FDA also supervises clinical trials, evaluations for the safety and effectiveness of drugs not yet approved by the FDA. When a drug is approved by the FDA, it is given an *indication* for use, meaning that the drug is approved for use to treat a particular disorder or condition based on data from clinical trials. The following are medications that are FDA indicated for use in treating ADD:

- dextroamphetamine (Dexedrine)

- mixed amphetamine salts (Adderall, Adderall XR)

- lisdexamphetamine (Vyvanse)

- methylphenidate (Concerta, Metadate, Daytrana, and Ritalin)

- dexmethylphenidate (Focalin XR)

- atomoxetine (Strattera)

- guanfacine (Intuniv)

Amphetamines, dexmethylphenidate, and methylphenidate are stimulants, while atomoxetine and guanfacine are not.

When a medication is not FDA indicated for ADD, it means that the drug companies are not allowed to advertise that medication as a treatment for ADD. However, your doctor may prescribe these medications for you. The following medications are not FDA indicated for treating ADD but may still be effective in treating it:

- bupropion (Wellbutrin XL)

- some tricyclic antidepressants

- clonidine (Catapres)

- modafinil (Provigil, Nuvigil)

STIMULANTS

Stimulants increase attention, decrease hyperactivity, and decrease impulsivity by stimulating the frontal lobe of the brain. The most noticeable side effects of stimulants are decreased appetite, stomachaches, and headaches. These are mostly temporary and may decrease in time.

Extended-release stimulants, such as Concerta, Adderall XR, Dexedrine Spansules, Vyvanse, and Daytrana, last from eight to twelve hours, making it more convenient to take the medications. You can take the extended-release stimulant before work or school, and it will be effective for most of the day. Immediate-release stimulants, such as Ritalin, Focalin, and Dexedrine, last three to four hours and are usually taken more than once a day.

Immediate Release	Extended Release
Ritalin	Concerta, Metadate CD, Ritalin LA
Adderall	Adderall XR
Dexedrine	Dexedrine Spansules
Focalin	Focalin XR
—	Vyvanse
—	Daytrana

Stimulants are classified as *Schedule II* medications by the FDA. This means that stimulant medications are "controlled substances," medications that have a mild addictive potential. Some people abuse stimulants for their side effects, such as increased alertness and weight loss. Because of the potential for abuse, stimulant medications cannot be called in to a pharmacy by your doctor. You have to pick up the prescription at the doctor's office.

Some people choose to stop their stimulant medication on weekends and holidays since they will not need to focus as much. However, keep in mind that ADD affects all aspects of your life—your job, social life, and relationships with family. Taking stimulant medication daily can give you a better total quality of life (Brown and Landgraf 2010; Spencer et al. 2008).

If you have to do any drug testing, make sure you tell the tester that you are taking a prescribed stimulant, and bring your medication bottle with you. Your test may be positive for amphetamines.

NONSTIMULANTS

Strattera

In 2002, Strattera became the first nonstimulant medication approved by the FDA for the treatment of ADD and the first medication approved for the treatment of adult ADD. Strattera works for adults, adolescents, and children. It is in a class of medications called selective norepinephrine reuptake inhibitors (SNRIs). This means that the medication allows more norepinephrine (a neurotransmitter) to linger in the spaces between neurons.

Strattera has been found to significantly decrease the severity of hyperactive and inattentive symptoms in adults when compared with a placebo (sugar pill) (Newcorn et al. 2008; Michelson et al. 2003). Strattera can be helpful for people who have not had success with stimulant medication or for those who have depression and anxiety in addition to ADD (Hammerness et al. 2009; Vaughan, Fegert, and Kratochvil 2009). Strattera is not addictive, so it's not a Schedule II drug like stimulant medications. Strattera can take two to six weeks to work, and the most common side effects of Strattera are stomach upset, dry mouth, and decreased appetite. Some of these side effects decrease with time. Strattera is effective twenty-four hours a day. The medication does not wear off; it stays in your system so you receive the full benefits. This means that Strattera must be taken every day.

Intuniv

In 2009, Intuniv (guanfacine) was approved by the FDA for the treatment of ADD. Intuniv interacts with receptors in the prefrontal cortex of the brain. Intuniv has been found to significantly reduce hyperactivity, impulsivity, and inattentiveness when compared with a placebo (sugar pill) (Biederman et al. 2008). Side effects include low blood pressure, low heart rate, fainting, and drowsiness. In addition, you may have to take Intuniv for up to two weeks before you see benefits.

OTHER MEDICATIONS

While Provigil (modafinil) and Wellbutrin XL (buproprion HCl extended release) are not currently FDA approved for the treatment of ADD, they have shown some effectiveness in treating the symptoms.

Provigil

Provigil (modafinil) is a long-acting stimulant used to help people with sleep disorders (such as narcolepsy) stay awake. It is not yet FDA approved for the treatment of adult ADD, but it may be helpful to adults with ADD who have not had success with other medications (Lindsay, Gudelsky, and Heaton 2006). A new, longer-lasting formulation of Provigil, called Nuvigil, was approved by the FDA in 2007 for the treatment of specific sleep disorders, including narcolepsy.

Wellbutrin XL

Wellbutrin XL (bupropion HCl extended release) is a norepinephrine and dopamine reuptake inhibitor (NDRI), an antidepressant. Like Strattera, Wellbutrin XL allows more norepinephrine to linger between the neurons. In addition, it also allows dopamine to share that space. Wellbutrin is FDA indicated for treating depression but not yet FDA indicated for treating ADD. However, this medication has shown promise in helping reduce ADD symptoms in adults (Wigal 2009; Solhkhah et al. 2005). Side effects include dry mouth, headaches, and nausea. In rare cases, seizures may occur, particularly in people who have a history of eating disorders.

HERBAL SUPPLEMENTS

Herbal supplements are pills or powders made from naturally occurring ingredients. Make sure you tell your doctor if you're considering taking herbal supplements or if you are already taking them. Some herbal supplements, including kava kava, valerian root, and St. John's wort, interact with your body's central nervous system and can also interact with your medication. Be aware that herbal supplements are not regulated by the FDA. For this reason, make sure the supplement's manufacturer adheres to strict quality-control measures. There is little scientific evidence that herbal supplements are effective in treating ADD (Sawni 2008).

Omega-3

There is evidence that omega-3 fatty acids can help improve the symptoms of ADD. Researchers have found that people with ADD have a significantly lower level of omega-3 in their blood (Schuchardt et al. 2010; Anatalis et al. 2006). Fish oil and polyunsaturated fatty acids, which contain omega-3 and omega-6, have been found to increase this level (Sinn and Bryan 2007; Young, Conquer, and Thomas 2005). ADD symptoms improved somewhat in children who were taking a combination of omega-3 and omega-6 supplements (Transler et al. 2010). Consult with your doctor before you begin taking any supplement, including omega-3.

Remembering to Take Your Medication

If you have ADD, it can be difficult to remember whether you took your medicine. Buy a seven-day pill container. This helps you remember to take your medicine and also prevents you from taking it twice. Fill the container at the beginning of the week, and always refill your pill container on the same day of the week. You can also set an alarm on your phone, create a recurring event on your phone's calendar, or get an app for your phone that will remind you when to take your medication. For suggestions on where to download medication-reminder apps, please see the resources listed at the end of this chapter.

Who Prescribes Medicine for ADD?

Psychiatrists, neurologists, and psychiatric nurse practitioners usually have specialized training in treating ADD. All physicians can prescribe medication, but you will find it easier to communicate with doctors who specialize in ADD. The doctor will interview you at length about your ADD symptoms and may use special tests to pinpoint your diagnosis. To track your progress, your doctor should use these assessments not only at your first visit but also at follow-up visits.

How to Find a Doctor

Go to the following resources and ask whom they recommend for prescribing adult ADD medication:

- an ADD support group

- your primary care physician

- online ADD forums

- relatives

- friends who have ADD

- parents of children who have ADD

- child psychiatrists

- psychotherapists who specialize in ADD

Your Doctor's Appointment

When you first go to a doctor who specializes in ADD, he or she will probably meet with you for about an hour. The doctor will most likely ask you about the following topics:

- the biggest problem you are having right now

- current and past symptoms of ADD

- eating and sleeping habits

- medical history (current medicines, drug allergies, history of seizures or head injury)

- family history of ADD, depression, anxiety, substance abuse, bipolar disorder, or schizophrenia

- educational history

- legal problems

- work history

The doctor asks you about all of these things to evaluate you thoroughly. The doctor wants an accurate *baseline*, a picture of you before you begin treatment. The more information you provide, the better. The baseline picture helps doctors determine how effective a treatment is for you.

It helps to have some of this information written down before your visit. The exercise at the end of this chapter will help you do this. Also bring in any paperwork you feel could help the doctor: previous medical records, letters from significant others regarding their concerns about your behavior, report cards and discipline reports from when you were a child, and previous psychological testing. It's a good idea to bring a significant other to your appointment. Studies have shown that people with ADD have difficulty judging their own behavior and that significant others may describe them more accurately (Quinlan 2000).

While you are at the doctor's office, they may have you fill out some questionnaires about adult ADD, such as the Conners Adult ADD Rating Scales (CAARS), the Attention Deficit Scale for Adults (ADSA), the Adult ADHD Self-Report Scale (ASRS), the Current Symptoms Scale, and the Childhood Symptoms Scale (Kessler et al. 2005; Conners, Erhardt, and Sparrow 1999; Barkley and Murphy 1998; Triolo and Murphy 1996). Some of the scales the clinician fills out as he talks with you, such as the ADHD Rating Scale IV (ADHD-RS-IV), the Brown Attention-Deficit Disorder Scales, and the Wender Utah Scale (DuPaul et al. 1998; Brown 1996; Ward, Wender, and Reimherr 1993). Be as honest and open as possible. As I've mentioned, the more information you give your clinician, the more he or she can help you. The doctor may also have you take a computerized test, such as the Integrated Visual and Auditory CPT (IVA+Plus™) (Sanford and Turner 2004).

This type of test measures your verbal and auditory attention capabilities.

Listen to your gut feeling when meeting with a doctor. You should feel that your questions were answered and the doctor conducted a thorough evaluation. It is perfectly acceptable to ask questions. Beware of doctors who do not like being asked about their methods of treatment. If you feel that your questions were not answered to your satisfaction, you have the right to seek a second opinion.

Keep in mind that the medications may take a while to work. Your doctor may also have to change your medications to find the one that works best for you. If something doesn't feel right, meet with another doctor for a second opinion. ADD is a chronic disorder, and you may need to work with your doctor over the long haul. It's worthwhile to take the time to find someone with whom you feel comfortable.

If you don't agree with something the clinician said or did during your appointment, the best way to handle this is to mention your concern to him or her while you are still at your appointment. If, after talking to the clinician, your concerns are not answered to your satisfaction, you have a few other options. First, you can get a second opinion from another clinician. However, if you feel the clinician has violated ethics or laws, you can contact the clinician's professional organization or the state licensing board. Again, the important thing is that you talk to the clinician first before taking these other measures.

Exercise: Help Your Doctor Help You

First appointments can make you nervous, so the more prepared you are, the better. Complete the "First Visit Notes" form on the next page and bring it with you. This will help you remember what you want to tell the doctor.

First Visit Notes

Name _____ Date _____

Why I am here today:

What I would like to accomplish at this visit:

What I would like to accomplish by taking medication:

Current medications (if any):

Name of medication	Dosage	When I take it
1.		
2.		
3.		
4.		
5.		
6.		

Medications I am allergic to:

Other doctors or counselors I have seen about my ADD and their contact information:

Medications I have taken in the past for ADD and any side effects I had:

In this chapter, you learned about the medications available for the treatment of ADD. In the next chapter, you will learn how to reduce clutter and get organized.

Resources

MEDICATION LOGS AND PILL REMINDERS

BBSmart Alarms Pro
www.blackberrysmart.com/alarmspro.php
(for Blackberry)

MedCoach
www.greatcall.com/MedCoach
(for iPhone)

MobiHand Pill Reminder
www.mobihand.com
(for Blackberry)

MEDICATION WEBSITES

Adderall XR
www.adderallxr.com

Daytrana
www.daytrana.com

Intuniv
www.intuniv.com

Strattera
www.strattera.com

Vyvanse
www.vyvanse.com

OTHER MEDICATION AND TREATMENT RESOURCES

Centerwatch
www.centerwatch.com

National Institute of Mental Health
www.nimh.nih.gov

U.S. Food and Drug Administration
www.fda.gov

3

Reduce Clutter and Get Organized

It may be difficult to precisely define clutter, but you know it when you see it. You may have items on your desk that you do not use, but they take up space. You may have papers on the floor of your office because you do not know what to do with them. Clutter in your home or work environment can make you feel overwhelmed and unproductive. In this chapter, you will learn some ADD-friendly ways to reduce your clutter and get organized.

Pace Yourself

People with ADD can wear themselves out by trying to tackle too much at once. This leads to burnout and avoidance of organization tasks. The key is to pace yourself. Think of decluttering as a series of short sprints instead of a marathon. Declutter and organize one drawer or surface at a time and work in blocks of time.

Set a timer for twenty minutes when you are organizing. Stop when the timer goes off. Don't fall into the trap of doing "just one more thing." Take a break and reward yourself for a job well done.

Work with an Organization Buddy

An organization buddy is a friend, relative, or coworker who assists you while you sort through papers, pay bills, clean out a closet, or complete any other organization task. Some people with ADD have problems with motivation but can focus relatively well. Others have difficulty in both areas. How much involvement you need from your organization buddy depends on the intensity of your ADD, your personal style, your organizational skills, and the task at hand.

PLAN A

Some people choose plan A, having an organization buddy who is in the room with them but does not interact with them. Sometimes just having someone nearby while you get organized can help you stay focused. For example, you may be sorting through papers, while your organization buddy is in the room but doing a separate activity. Plan A is good for people who feel they need a little help with organization but have a good idea of how they would like things organized.

PLAN B

Others choose plan B, having their organization buddy help out but not give advice or suggestions. If you are sorting through papers, you hand the papers to your organization buddy and tell her where you want her to put the papers. Organization buddies can help you label boxes, get trash bags, or do any other tasks that help you organize more efficiently. For example, you are going through your closet. You decide that you will donate any unwanted clothing to the local domestic violence shelter. You tell your organization buddy to make a box labeled "shelter." When you find an item you no longer need, you tell your organization buddy and hand it to her. She puts it in the box. This make the process go faster and reduces the possibility of distractions. Plan B is preferable for people who have a fairly good idea of how they want to be organized but have more difficulties staying focused.

PLAN C

In plan C, your organization buddy actively participates in the process. He suggests ways to organize items, asks you whether you really need a particular item, and redirects you when you lose focus. For example, you decide to organize your kitchen cupboards. Your organization buddy takes out each item and asks you if you want to keep it, throw it out, or give it away. He then places the item in the appropriate pile. You do not even touch the items. This reduces your level of distraction and your ambivalence about getting rid of items. This option is for people who need help finding a plan for organization and tend to lose focus frequently.

For some projects, you may have a clear idea of what you would like to accomplish. You may want to go with plan A or plan B. For other projects, you may feel that you don't know where to start. In this situation, you may want to go with plan C. You can use an organization buddy in different ways for different tasks.

Before you begin a task, tell your organization buddy what level of involvement you need so that both of you have a clear understanding of expectations. It reduces frustration and increases efficiency for both of you.

FIND AN ORGANIZATION BUDDY

When looking for an organization buddy, think of your friends, relatives, and coworkers who don't have ADD and do have time to help you out. Look for people who are

- organized

- patient

- accepting of your ADD and your lack of organizational skills

- able to tell if you are getting frustrated or burned out

- good at managing time

- good at listening

If you can't find a friend or relative who would be a good organization buddy, a professional organizer can help. Make sure she understands the chronic disorganization that is a part of ADD. Ask her if she has worked with clients with ADD before. She needs to be flexible and able to work with different organization styles. Remember, you are the expert on what works for you.

Also consider hiring a *personal assistant*. This is someone who comes to your house a few hours every week to help you with light cleaning, organizing, and errands. To find a personal assistant, seek recommendations from your family and friends. You can also place an ad online. Make sure you ask for a résumé and references, and complete a background check before you hire anyone.

COMPENSATE YOUR ORGANIZATION BUDDY

How you compensate your organization buddy depends on your relationship. If you have a business relationship with your organization buddy, you might want to consider paying him. Professional organizers are always paid.

If you have a personal relationship, you may want to consider bartering services. For example, your organization buddy can barter her time for a skill you have, such as helping her paint her house. Agree upon these details before working together. It is important to compensate your organization buddy in some way because she will be spending a lot of time and effort helping you.

Reduce Visual Stress

Clutter creates *visual stress*, a feeling of chaos and lack of motivation caused by an overload of stimuli in your environment. While eliminating clutter is ideal, it is not always realistic for people with ADD. Covering up your clutter is a quick way to reduce your visual stress. Have an empty trunk in your family room. If company comes over unexpectedly, dump the clutter into the trunk. Just make a note that you put the items in the trunk. Choose wall units and other furniture with doors you can shut when you are not using the items inside. Just by shutting doors on wall units and shelves, you immediately reduce the amount of visual stress in your home. You will feel less overwhelmed when your clutter "disappears."

The Law of Usage

When you keep items you no longer use, they just take up space, and they eventually become damaged or destroyed. Look at the stuff around your house. Are there items you have not used in over a year? Whom do you know who could really use these items? Are there charities that would benefit from this item? By giving away these unused items, you not only help the recipient, you also help yourself. You also give that item a new lease on life.

Explore Feng Shui

Feng shui (pronounced "fung shway") is the ancient Chinese art of placement. The energy of life, or *chi*, is a fundamental principle of feng shui. Chi is all around you, but it can become blocked, causing you to feel depressed or anxious or even making you sick. Using the principles of feng shui, you can change your living space to improve the flow of chi. A good flow of chi results in better health, finances, and relationships.

Although you may not believe in the principles underlying feng shui, the practical tips are interesting and very effective at reducing clutter. It is a fun and intellectually stimulating way for people with ADD to get organized. The principles of feng shui can help you focus better by making your environment less chaotic and more peaceful. Feng shui can also help you feel more at home in your environment.

One principle of feng shui is that clutter stops you from letting go and moving on to new things. Clutter can make you feel like you are in a rut because it blocks your chi. Clearing off surfaces is a good first step toward decluttering your environment and moving on with the organization process.

Use the Five-Box Method for Sorting Items

Tackling clutter can be overwhelming. In one drawer, you may find an item that needs to be returned to your neighbor, another item that needs to be donated, and another item that belongs in a different room. How do you go about decluttering and keep it simple at the same time? The answer is the five-box method, a streamlined process for tackling clutter. The simpler the decluttering process is, the easier it will be to follow through. To begin, get four large boxes, one large garbage bag, and a permanent marker.

- Label the first box "Fix It." Put items in this box that are not working properly and are repairable. Before putting an item in this box, ask yourself if repairing the item is worth your time and money.

- Label the second box "Give It Away." This box is for items that would be enjoyed or used more by a charitable organization or by your family or friends.

- Label the third box "Keep It." This box is for items that are in good working order and have been used in the past year. This box is also for items that have sentimental value.

- Label the fourth box "Don't Know." Use this box if you are unsure if you need an item. Put this box away for a year. If you did not use the item during that time, you probably do not need it.

- The fifth "box" is your garbage bag. The garbage bag is for items that are broken and nonrepairable or items that do not have value to you or anyone else. When the bag is full, put it in your trash can.

Sort through your belongings and put them in the appropriate box. Try to categorize the items as quickly but as thoughtfully as possible. The longer you hold on to an item, the harder it is to let it go.

Organize Your Papers

Papers can get out of control quickly. While you should be working toward becoming as paperless as possible, here is a method for taming the paper monster. Buy a file cart with wheels. You are more likely to file a paper if you can just pull the cart over to you instead of getting up and walking to the cart. Also buy some hanging file folders. Label five folders as follows.

Read It. This folder is for articles and papers you want to read. Bring this folder along when you have appointments and will be waiting awhile. It is amazing how much reading can be accomplished while you wait.

File It. This folder is for papers you need for future reference, such as legal documents, warranties, and receipts. Schedule a time every month to file the papers in this folder. Otherwise, you'll end up with a very full folder. Doing a little at a time gets a lot more accomplished.

Take Action. This folder is for bills and other paperwork that require immediate attention.

Give Away. This folder is for articles and other papers that are of more use or interest to someone else.

Don't Know. Use this file for papers you're not sure you need.

Once a month, revisit your file cart. Look in the "Don't Know" file. Have you used these papers in the past month? If not, either file them or throw them out. Is there anything left in the "Give Away" folder? If so, mail it and get it out of your house. Look in the "Take Action" folder. What is left in this folder? Do it today, file it, or throw it out. If you find papers that you will need in the upcoming months, continue reading this chapter to discover a way to keep track of those papers.

Keep Track of Important Papers

Being able to find the papers you need when you need them saves you time and frustration. Buy two accordion folders, one preprinted with the days of the month and another preprinted with the months of the year. The folder with the days of the month is for papers you will need this month. If you need a car wash coupon for next Saturday, file it under next Saturday's date. The folder with the months of the year is for papers you will need in the upcoming months. If you receive an invitation for a party two months from now, file it under the month of the event. At the end of each month, go through both folders. If you have papers left over from that month, transfer them to next month's pockets, or throw them away if you no longer need them.

Buy One, Replace One

When you buy something, donate or throw out a similar item. For example, if you get a new book, donate one of your other books to your local public library or to a school library. This technique eliminates the growth of clutter in your home. You also reduce the amount of work in the long run.

Cut Household Clutter

Clutter around your home can build up fast. It is almost like a snowball going down a hill, getting bigger and bigger with time. One of the best ways to reduce clutter is to cut it off at its source—become as paperless as possible.

CHECK OUT THE LIBRARY AND E-BOOKS

Instead of buying books that you never look at again, go to your local library and check them out for free. Your tax money helped pay for the library, so get a return on your investment. By using your library, you save money and avoid adding to the books collecting dust at home. If you're an avid reader, consider reading e-books. Many classics are free in e-book format because they are in the public domain (this means the copyright has run out on them). Sometimes newer titles are available because the author wants more people to have access to the work. You don't necessarily need to purchase a wireless reading device—you can read e-books right on your laptop. Resources for e-books can be found at the end of this chapter.

SIGN UP FOR ELECTRONIC BILLS AND STATEMENTS

Many companies give you the option of receiving your bills via e-mail and paying them on the Internet. Some even offer incentives to switch to electronic billing. By receiving electronic bills, you greatly reduce the mail you receive. You may forget to pay a paper bill that you left on your desk, but you are more likely to pay electronic bills immediately. You will learn more about electronic money management in chapter 6.

REDUCE YOUR JUNK MAIL

Cutting back the amount of junk mail you receive greatly reduces your clutter. It also reduces the time it takes you to sort through your mail. When you give your name and address to companies, your contact information may be entered into a national database. Companies pay for the names on this list for marketing purposes. For information on how to opt out of receiving junk mail and preapproved credit card offers, see the end of this chapter.

Do not fill out any warranty or product registration cards. Companies use this information to compile mailing lists. Many companies have opt-out policies, allowing you to request that they not distribute your information to anyone. Always choose this option.

GO THROUGH YOUR MAIL AS SOON AS YOU GET IT

Stand by a trash can as you go through your mail. Immediately throw out any catalogs, junk mail, and ads. If mail arrives for a family member, place it in a basket. While I recommend that you receive online bills only, if you do receive a paper bill, put it in a separate bill-paying basket. This basket is described in detail in chapter 6.

Keep Your Bag Organized

Find a briefcase or purse with many compartments. Some have key rings attached, and some even have a light built in so you can see the contents. A bag with compartments helps you find a place for everything. Buy a wallet in a bright color so you can locate it more easily in your bag. Do not change bags too often, or you may lose important items.

Clear zippered bags are a great way to compartmentalize items in your purse or attaché case. Put your personal care items, such as medications, in one bag. Put pens and pencils in another. If you travel frequently, clear bags can help speed up your security check at the airport—screeners can more easily see your bag's contents.

Declutter Your Closet

Closets are like the black hole of your house. Some items go into closets and never see the light of day again. You may have clothes that you haven't worn since high school and that don't fit you anymore. You may have bought multiples of the same shirt because you forgot you already had one. Your hangers may be a tangled mess, and you may not have room for all your shoes. Sound familiar? Here are some ideas for taming the closet monster.

START WITH A FRESH CLOSET

Go through your closet and take out the clothes you have not worn in the past year. Look at every piece of clothing you have taken out of your closet. Consider:

- Does the item still fit you?

- Does the item have sentimental value?

- Will you need this item in the future?

If not, donate it or give it away. Now you are ready to tackle the rest of the closet black hole.

ORGANIZE YOUR CLOTHING BY TYPE

Group the clothes in your closet according to the following categories:

- shirts

- jackets and blazers

- pants

- shorts

- dresses

- skirts

If you have a suit, hang the blazer and pants separately. You may find that you can mix and match the pieces and create even more outfits.

USE YOUR CLOSET SPACE EFFICIENTLY

Make the best use of your closet space. Grouping items by type reduces visual clutter and makes it easier to find things. Toss out your wire hangers and use wood or plastic hangers instead. Specialty hangers for belts, ties, and even jewelry can help save space. Get your shoes off the closet floor using a cubby, rack, or over-the-door organizer.

USE SPACE BAGS

Space Bags are plastic storage bags that can become airtight. Connect your vacuum hose to the bag, and all of the air is removed. You then have your items stored in a compact package. Space Bags are great for storing winter clothes, such as sweaters, gloves, and coats. Space Bags are also available in a travel size that does not require the use of a vacuum hose.

STREAMLINE CLOTHES SHOPPING

Before you go out shopping, make a list of what you need, and stick to this list. The next time you feel you need some "retail therapy," buy an accessory instead of another piece of clothing. Accessories can help you create several outfits out of a few pieces of clothing. Determine which colors look best on you. Knowing which colors to wear and which to avoid makes your shopping expedition much more efficient. It also reduces the amount of unused clothing in your closet.

Exercise: Rethink Organization

Many people with ADD have experienced negative reactions from others regarding their lack of organization.

- Have you been criticized or disciplined for being messy or disorganized?

- How have these experiences affected your feelings about getting organized?

- What would you like to change about your views of organization?

Once you have determined what you would like to change, start making a plan. What do you need to make this change?

- Do you need to read up on organization strategies?

- Do you need to talk with other adults with ADD about their experiences with organization?

- Do you need to talk to a counselor?

- How will you go about contacting these people or obtaining this information?

Exercise: Find the Organizational Hot Spots in Your Home

It can be overwhelming to start decluttering and organizing your home. This exercise will help you tackle the areas that need the most organizational help.

Which areas of the house cause you the most difficulties due to clutter and messiness? Write down the names of these rooms or areas. For each room, answer the following questions:

- What is your biggest problem with this room?

- What can you never find in this room?

- Have you tried to organize this room before? What were the results?

- What could you do differently this time to feel more successful?

- Do you have a lot of things you don't need in this room, or do they just need to be grouped with similar items and stored more efficiently?

Now that you know what needs to be fixed, it is time to create goals and deadlines for each room. If you could wave a magic wand and make this room exactly the way you wanted it to be, what would it look like? Would you have fewer items in the room? Would you add another piece of furniture for storage? The ideas you come up with are now your goals for the room.

Next, decide on the steps and deadlines for each room. For example, one of your goals for your home office is to get rid of some of your books. Your goal, steps, and deadlines would look like this:

Goal: Decrease the number of books in the home office.

Steps:

1. Get two boxes: one for books to donate and one for books to give away to friends and family.
   Deadline: By this Saturday.

2. Go through one bookshelf at a time and take out all the books I have not used in the past five years.
   Deadline: One bookshelf a week.

3. Sort through the books and put them in the appropriate box.
    Deadline: One week for all the books.

4. Give the books to the donation center or to friends or family.
    Deadline: Two days after sorting through all the books.

The deadlines you create are your best estimate of how long it will take you to accomplish each step. You are the best judge of how long it takes you to do something. Be realistic. Also, do not make your goals so open ended that you have difficulties getting motivated. People with ADD work better in small steps. By creating manageable steps and reasonable deadlines, you can reach your goals.

In this chapter, you have learned how to reduce your visual clutter and pare down your belongings. The key is to declutter gradually. You do not need to do it all at once. You have had clutter for years, and it will not disappear overnight. Reward yourself for your progress, even if you consider it to be a small step forward.

Excessive clutter can lead to another phenomenon: losing your belongings. In the next chapter, you will learn how to not be such a "loser."

Resources

Kolberg, J., and K. Nadeau. 2002. *ADD-Friendly Ways to Organize Your Life*. New York: Routledge.

Morgenstern, J. 2009. *SHED Your Stuff, Change Your Life: A Four-Step Guide to Getting Unstuck*. New York: Fireside.

Morgenstern, J. 2004. *Organizing from the Inside Out: The Foolproof System for Organizing Your Home, Your Office and Your Life*, 2nd ed. New York: Holt Paperbacks.

Direct Marketing Association
www.dmachoice.org

Federal Trade Commission
"Unsolicited Mail, Telemarketing, and Email: Where to Go to 'Just Say No'"
www.ftc.gov/bcp/edu/pubs/consumer/alerts/alt063.shtm

Kindle Wireless Reading Device
www.amazon.com

National Association of Professional Organizers
www.napo.net
15000 Commerce Parkway
Suite C
Mount Laurel, NJ 08054
Tel: (856) 380-6828
Fax: (856) 439-0525
E-mail: napo@napo.net

OptOutPrescreen
Opt out of credit card and insurance offers
www.optoutprescreen.com

Professional Organizers Online
www.professionalorganizersonline.com

Project Gutenberg Free E-Books
www.gutenberg.org

Space Bags
www.spacebag.com

Stacks and Stacks
www.stacksandstacks.com

4

Stop Being a "Loser"

A common trait of people with ADD is the uncanny ability to lose things. How many times have you lost your keys, phone, glasses, or important papers? Have you ever stayed up late trying to find something or been late to work because you couldn't find your keys? Losing things costs you time and money.

A Place for Everything and Everything in Its Place

When items have a home, it is much easier to remember where they go and to make the effort to put them there.

POINT OF USAGE

It is a lot easier to find things when you store them near their *point of usage*. The point of usage is the location where you are most likely to use the item. For example, if you use your reading glasses when you read in bed, keep your glasses on your nightstand. Choosing the most convenient location for an item means you are more likely to put it back there.

LINE OF SIGHT

A corollary to the point of usage is the *line of sight*. When storing items on shelves, put the most frequently used items at eye level. This makes them easier to find. For example, in the kitchen, put the spices that you use on a daily basis on the cupboard shelf that is at eye level. Less frequently used spices can go on a higher shelf.

GROUP SIMILAR ITEMS TOGETHER

Storing similar items together increases your chances of finding things when you need them. You can group items using containers and dividers.

Clear containers are best because you can see the contents. Choose containers that have a pull-out drawer rather than a lid so you don't have to unstack the containers to get to the one you want.

Label your containers with stickers or a labeling machine. If you are labeling a box, put a list of the contents on each side so you can tell what is in the box when it is on a shelf.

Dividers keep items separate and secure. Divider trays can be placed in desk drawers to organize office supplies.

Dividers in storage containers can protect items like Christmas ornaments.

FIND A HOME FOR YOUR STUFF

Jump right in and take a look at what you own. Pull out a drawer and look at the contents. Ask yourself

- How often do I use this item?

- Where do I use it the most?

- Is there a better location for this item?

- Are there similar items to store with this item?

Gather together similar items that are used in the same location. Put them in a box and carry them to the place where you use them the most. Get rid of items you have not used in the past year. Sort through only one drawer or cupboard at a time. Remember to take breaks, especially if you start to feel frustrated.

Keep Track of Tricky Items

Here are some practical ways to hang on to items that are especially easy to lose.

HOLD ON TO YOUR KEYS

Keys can be your worst nightmare. Put a key rack or basket by the entry door of your home. Place your keys there as soon as you come in the door. Make sure that the keys are out of reach of small children and pets. Consider getting a key chain with a transponder that beeps and/or has a flashing light. Press a button on a homing device and your keys respond. Wear your keys on a wristband or lariat when you are out. It may not be the latest fashion statement, but you will be able to find your keys.

Keyless entry locks are an alternative. You install a keypad on a door and enter a code to unlock the door. You can find keyless entry locks at home improvement stores.

Make Two Copies of Your Keys

When you have two sets of keys, you increase your chances of getting into your house safe and sound. Keep one set of keys in your wallet and give another set to a friend. Do not leave spare keys under your doormat. This is one of the first places burglars look.

ID Your Keys

Instead of putting your name and address on your keys or other valuable items, sign up for a service that assigns you a code for your items. Attach the code and the company's contact information to your key ring either with a tag or sticker. A person who finds your keys can contact the company and give them the code. The company then calls you, or, depending on the service, the finder can mail your keys to the company at no cost to him or her. For more information, see the resources listed at the end of this chapter.

WHERE ARE YOUR GLASSES?

If you use your sunglasses mostly for driving, get a clip that attaches to your visor. Keep your sunglasses in the car. Also get a cord for your sunglasses. If you need to take your sunglasses off, they stay with you.

It is difficult to find your glasses when you can't see them. Get a tray for your glasses that you keep next to your bed. Put your glasses there every night. Buy a brightly colored case for your glasses so they are easy to spot.

KEEP A HOLD ON YOUR PHONE

You may have noticed that your phone "disappears" or gets damaged more often than other people's. A phone and a person with ADD do not always mix. Here is a small piece of hardware you are expected to hold on to for a long time. Not so easy, is it?

Always keep your phone in the same zippered pocket in your bag. Many bags have a compartment especially made for phones. Buy a phone case with a clip so you can attach it to the pocket in your bag. That way, if your bag gets tipped over, your phone won't fall out. You can use a belt clip for your phone if you do not carry a bag.

Always keep your phone charger in the same visible location in your home. Keep your charger off the floor. It is very easy to step on if it is in your path. You can also get a container that holds all your electronic devices together for recharging.

PROTECT YOUR CREDIT CARDS

Photocopy or scan both sides of all your credit cards. Make sure you can see the customer service phone numbers clearly on your photocopy. When using your credit card, keep the card in your sight the entire time. Keep your wallet open in your hands. Ask for your card back as soon as the cashier has swiped it. If you have lost your credit cards, immediately call the card companies. If losing credit cards is a continual problem, get a prepaid credit card or lower your credit limit. This way, if your card is stolen or lost, there is a lower limit to how much a thief can charge on your card.

If you are purchasing items online, don't use a credit card that is in any way attached to your bank account. Consider getting a prepaid credit card that you use just for online purchases, and make sure your computer has antivirus and spyware protection.

HOLD ON TO YOUR JEWELRY

Losing jewelry can be heartbreaking and expensive. When you take your jewelry off at night, put it in a small container on your nightstand. You can also use a hanging jewelry organizer. These eliminate tangling and allow you to see all of your jewelry at once.

KEEP YOUR SOCKS MATED FOR LIFE

If you have a Bermuda Sock Triangle in your home, now there is hope. Sock Locks are small rubber discs that keep your sock pairs together when you are not wearing them. They can go through the washer and dryer. Information on Sock Locks can be found at the end of this chapter.

If you find some socks without partners, keep them in a bag in the sock drawer. The next time you find another lonely sock, look in the bag for its mate. If you haven't found mates for the socks in a few weeks, throw the odd socks out. Also try to buy the same type of socks—less searching for a match!

HOLD ON TO YOUR WINTER WEAR

Buy multiple pairs of the same glove. If you lose a glove, you have a replacement handy. If you take off your gloves while you are out, stuff them securely into the inside pockets of your jacket. When you come home, toss your gloves and hat into a basket by the door. To prevent children from losing mittens, use mitten clips to clip the mittens to the jacket sleeve. Keep an over-the-door shoe organizer in your closet, and store your gloves and hats in it.

MAKE PEACE WITH YOUR CAR

Keep your auto registration papers and a copy of your insurance card in the glove compartment. If you need to keep track of your mileage, keep a small notebook in your glove compartment. Even better, you can get an app for your phone that keeps track of your mileage (see the resources section for suggestions). Also keep jumper cables, a first aid kit, and a flashlight with extra batteries in your car.

People with ADD can have difficulties remembering where they parked. To make it easier to find your car in a parking lot, tie a bright ribbon onto the antenna. Write down where you parked, either on a notepad or on your phone's calendar. Park your car in the same location each time you use that parking lot. Before you drive off, check the roof, hood, and trunk to make sure you haven't left anything on top.

PREVENT LUGGAGE MISHAPS

Traveling and adjusting to a new environment is stressful enough for a person with ADD. Avoid the added stress of losing your luggage. Buy luggage in an unusual color or pattern. Attach a colorful sticker or ID tag to your bag, and put contact information on the outside and inside of your luggage. When your bag is unique, it is easier to spot on the baggage carousel, and it's less likely that another passenger will take your bag by mistake. If your bag does not show up on the baggage carousel, tell airline staff immediately. However, an even easier way of keeping track of your bag is to do carry-on baggage only. It may also save you money, as many airlines are now charging fees for every checked bag.

Pack toiletries, medications, a change of clothes, and important documents in your carry-on bag. Also carry on any valuable items, such as a laptop or jewelry. If your luggage is lost, at least you will feel more relaxed knowing you have some essential items. Always keep your car keys in your carry-on bag. To ensure a speedier security screening, pack items in your carry-on bag in clear plastic bags. That way airport security can see everything in your bag, and it is packed in a more organized fashion. There are also TSA-approved laptop bags that don't require a passenger to take his or her laptop out of the bag for security. Any time that you're freed of an extra step means that you are more likely to hold on to your item.

Establish Rituals

Going through the same routine each day can help you save time and avoid losing things. Write out the steps you take getting ready in the morning and then laminate that list. Use a dry-erase marker to cross through the items as you go. Items on your daily routine list may include:

- Eat breakfast

- Take shower

- Get dressed

- Feed kids

- Put lunches in kids' backpacks

- Drive kids to school

PREPARE FOR THE NEXT DAY

Keep a small tray in your bedroom. At the end of the day, put your wallet, money clip, phone, and any other items you carry with you in the tray. Leaving in the morning is much easier when you have all your necessary items in one location.

Spend fifteen minutes every night picking up and putting things away before you go to bed. Fifteen minutes may not seem like a lot of time, but the overall effect adds up.

Also, lay out your entire outfit for the next day. Repair any missing buttons. Preparing an outfit the night before prevents a last-minute rush to find your shoes or cuff links. This is especially helpful for night owls who have difficulty thinking clearly in the morning. If you have to iron your clothes, do it the night before and then hang them up. Better yet, buy wrinkle-free garments.

CHECK YOURSELF BEFORE YOU LEAVE

When you are leaving your home, stop before you close the door and check that you have your wallet, keys, planner, and phone with you. Make a list of these essential items. Laminate it so it lasts longer and post it by the door. Also carry a pocket-size laminated list of these items. Establish a ritual of checking your list before you leave work or any other location. You can also set a daily reminder on your phone with a list of items that you need to take with you.

Keep Track of Your Kids

Losing your gloves or your phone is annoying, but losing your child is terrifying and dangerous. It can be easy to lose your kids in a crowded public place, especially if they have ADD and are distractible and prone to wandering. If you are going to be in a crowded place, dress your child in bright colors so she is easy to locate.

If you lose your child in a mall or store, time is of the essence. Immediately tell the staff that your child is missing. Many stores have a policy of immediately locking their doors when a child is missing. If the store does not have this policy, demand that they place security personnel at the entry and exit doors. Carry a current photo of your child with information about her weight, height, and distinguishing features, such as scars and birthmarks.

Yell your child's name loudly while you are looking for her. The more people who know your child is missing, the more quickly she will be found. Have an up-to-date photo of your child on your phone or on your person at all times. Teach your child to go to a customer service counter or tell an employee if she is lost. Think of where your child would go. Does she have a favorite store? Was she asking to go somewhere?

If your child tends to run off, use a cord that connects your child's wrist to your wrist or belt loop. You can also get a harness for your child. People may stare at you, but it is better than losing your child.

Global positioning system (GPS) technology allows you to determine a person's exact location in the world. There are small GPS devices that can be placed in a child's backpack or on a key ring. You can view the location of the GPS device and get tracking updates online. For more information on these devices, see the end of this chapter.

Recently, there have been incidents of parents accidentally leaving their child in the car while they went to work (Null 2011). Whereas babies were previously required to sit facing backward for only a few months, now states mandate that they must be in backward-facing car seats until they are much bigger. If you're unaccustomed to dropping your child at day care, you might do your usual routine and forget that your child is in the car when you park. One recommendation is to put your purse or phone near your child's car seat. While you may not take your child to day care every morning before work, you do take your purse or phone with you every day—you are "programmed" to remember those items. This is especially important for people with ADHD, who have difficulty deviating from a structured routine and are prone to forgetfulness.

Prevent the Loss of a Pet

Make sure your pet wears a tag with your current contact information. Put your e-mail, phone number, and address on the tag. Your pet also needs a current rabies tag. Lost pets without rabies tags may be quarantined, delaying their return.

ID microchips are available for pets. The microchip is about the size of a grain of rice, and it contains all of your contact information. The microchip is injected painlessly under your pet's skin by a veterinary professional. Many veterinary offices and animal control centers have scanners that can read the microchip. They can then contact you using the information on the chip (as long as you keep that contact information current). Even if your pet has a microchip, keep a current identification tag on your pet's collar. Contact your veterinarian or animal control center about obtaining the microchip. You can also have a GPS device attached to your pet's collar or identification tag. More information on microchipping and GPS tracking devices can be found at the end of this chapter.

When walking your dog, use a standard leash instead of a retractable leash. Retractable leashes are more difficult to hold on to and can snap if your dog runs.

If your pet is lost, let as many people as possible know. Make a flyer with a current photo of your pet and include his name, age, breed, and size. Adding a cute photo of your pet with a child increases your chances of having your pet returned to you. List your phone numbers and your e-mail so people have different ways of contacting you. Visit your local animal control center daily to see if your pet has been turned in as a stray. Also turn to the power of the Internet to post information about your lost pet. The more people who know your pet is missing, the more likely your pet will be spotted (no pun intended). By using Facebook or Twitter or sending a mass e-mail, you can post a picture of your pet and the location where he went missing. Also list your e-mail, phone numbers, and state if you're offering a reward. There are also websites where you can post information on your lost pet. See the end of this chapter for more information. Most important, have your pets spayed or neutered. This reduces their desire to escape your yard looking for love.

What to Do When You Lose Something

If you have ADD, you can get overwhelmed quickly. Then you may shut down and not be able to function. Here are some ways to make things easier on yourself when you lose something.

Keep it in perspective. People without ADD lose things, too. You just do it more often. In the scheme of life, losing an item is small compared to a loss of health or life.

Repeat a phrase to yourself. Say to yourself over and over, "I will find this item." Positive thinking can go a long way. Some people say a prayer to the patron saint of lost items, Saint Anthony. Asking Saint Anthony for help has worked for Catholics and non-Catholics alike.

Retrace your steps. Where were you during the day? Go back to those locations or call them and describe the item in detail. Also take advantage of the Internet to locate lost items by using social networking websites to let your friends know you're looking for an item.

Know when to take a break. If you are getting very frustrated, you probably will not find your item. Sit back and rest. Taking a break can help you think of new places to look.

Exercise: What Do You Lose the Most?

What item do you find yourself losing most often? Here is an exercise to figure out why you lose a particular item and then to learn strategies to avoid losing it in the future.

First, try to remember how you usually lose this item.

- Does it fall out of your bag?

- Do you put it down somewhere and accidentally leave it?

- Do you put it in a special place in your house and then forget where you put it?

Once you have figured out how you are losing this item, you can brainstorm ideas about how you can prevent this item from being lost again. Think about products you can buy or changes in your routine or behaviors that can help keep this item in your possession.

If you lose items when they fall out of your bag, you may need to purchase a bag with zippered pockets or a key clip. If you put items down somewhere and then leave them, you may need to check that you have all your items with you before you leave. If you put items in a special place and then forget where you put them, you could make a cheat sheet that lists the storage location of different items.

By doing this exercise, you are pinpointing what you need to change and making a concrete plan. If you have difficulty coming up with ideas, review this chapter or ask an organized friend for tips.

In this chapter, you have learned techniques to avoid losing items. In the next chapter, you will learn how to prevent another kind of loss—the loss of time.

Resources

Amber Alert GPS
www.amberalertgps.com

Back To Ya
www.backtoya.com

Fido Finder
www.fidofinder.com

HomeAgain Pet Microchipping
www.homeagain.com

Key Rescue
www.key-rescue.com

KeyRinger
www.keyringer.com/

MileBug
http://milebug.com/

MileageManager
www.mileagemanager.com

Missing Pet Network/USDA Animal Care Office
www.missingpet.net/

Sock Locks
www.sock-locks.com

WorldTracker GPRS
www.trackingtheworld.com/wtgprs.htm

5

Manage Your Time

Managing time can be very difficult for people with ADD. In chapter 1, you read about the executive functions of the frontal lobe of the brain, which is impaired in people with ADD. One of these executive functions is the ability to manage time. If you have ADD, you may find that

- You make lists that you lose or never use.

- You write down appointments and phone numbers on sticky notes and then lose them.

- You are late to appointments because you did not give yourself enough time to get there.

- You forget appointments.

- You have constant interruptions that make it difficult for you to get back on track.

- You always check your phone immediately after it flashes or beeps.

These problems can drive you crazy and make your life more complicated.

Most time management books give tips that are time consuming, detailed, and difficult to follow. In this chapter, you will learn realistic time management strategies. You will learn about planners, master lists, effective use of your phone and e-mail, and the importance of delegating tasks. You will also learn how to choose the best possible time to do a task and how to make transitions smoothly.

Use a Paper Planner or Smartphone

A paper planner or smartphone is essential to the person with ADD. A paper planner or smartphone acts as your "external brain." You can use it to write down appointments, contact information, birthdays, and even ideas. The more you write in your paper planner or enter in your smartphone, the less you have to remember.

PAPER PLANNERS

Advantages	Disadvantages
Paper planners are available in a wide range of prices.	You need to photocopy the planner regularly in case it is lost.
They allow you to view an entire day or month at once.	If you lose your planner and have not made photocopies, you have lost all your information.
They are inexpensive to replace.	Erasures and changes can look messy.

SMARTPHONES

Advantages	Disadvantages
You can focus on one day, one week, or one month at a time.	You will need to learn how to use it.
You can delete information you do not need.	It costs more money than a paper planner.
You can choose from a variety of apps.	
You can download information onto a hard drive or online calendar.	They need to be recharged.

Smartphones have a calendar, contacts list, phone, camera, and Internet all in one device. The advantage is that you only have to remember and carry around one device. The disadvantage is that if you lose it, you have lost your calendar, phone, photos, and Internet access all at once. For guidance on choosing a smartphone, see the resources section at the end of this chapter.)

MAKE A COPY OR UPLOAD YOUR INFORMATION

If you have a paper planner, photocopy it often. Keep this copy in a separate location from your planner. If you have a smartphone, make sure you back up your calendar, contacts, and e-mails onto your laptop. You have the option of doing this wirelessly—you don't even have to connect your phone to your laptop. You can also automatically sync your calendar and contacts to an online site. If your laptop crashes or something happens to your phone, you will still have all your information online.

Use a Master List

Merely writing things down can help you remember them. When you think of things that need to be done, write them all down in a notebook, a specific area of your planner, or in a memo app on your smartphone. This is your master list: one location for all your to-do items. Use your master list to combine errands and save time. If you have to drop off the dry cleaning across town, check your master list to see if there is another errand to do on that same side of town.

. If you have messy handwriting (as is common when people have ADD), use a dictation app on your smartphone or laptop. Information on dictation apps and software can be found at the end of this chapter.

Set Deadlines

Setting deadlines for projects is very important for the person with ADD. When you create a "finish line," you are much more likely to follow through. When you have a large project, break it down and set several small deadlines. Reward yourself after meeting each deadline. If you have difficulty breaking projects into smaller steps, ask for help from a friend or organization buddy, as you read about in chapter 3.

Avoid Overscheduling

Sometimes, having too much unscheduled time can make you feel unmotivated. As a person with ADD, you may find that you accomplish much more when you have a busy schedule. However, a busy schedule can also overwhelm you. Remember, you can't be in two places at once.

One reason you may have too much on your schedule is that it is difficult to say no. It can be very hard to turn people down when they have asked you to do something. Do you say yes to too many activities and commitments? It is nice to be needed, but reducing stress is essential for your mental and physical health. You don't have to go into a lot of detail or make excuses. Just say, "I'm sorry, I can't do that" or "I'm sorry, that doesn't work for me."

Delegate Tasks

Let's face it—very few of us feel that we were put on earth to do laundry and wash dishes. Learning to delegate means asking other people to help you. Asking people to help is not a weakness. It is a sign that you are smart enough to know that a task does not make the best use of your skills and time. You may hesitate to delegate because you feel that no one will be able to do that task as well as you can. However, others are usually just as committed to doing a good job. You may also hesitate to pay someone to complete a task. Hiring someone may cost you money, but it will save time and aggravation in the long run.

LOOK INTO COACHING

ADD coaches can help you learn how to effectively schedule your time, prioritize tasks, and set goals. Coaches can also help you become more organized and find a method that works for you! You can get information on coaching services at the end of this chapter.

HAVE YOUR FAMILY HELP OUT

Children (including those with ADD) can help around the house. Do not expect children with ADD to do chores unsupervised. Younger children with ADD can do chores along with you, and older children with ADD will need you to stay in the room while they do their chores. Here are some suggestions for helping your children learn chores:

- Teach your child one chore at a time. Explain each step of the chore.

- Stay positive and patient. Praise is much more effective than criticism.

- Use a chore chart or reward system to keep your child motivated. However, the novelty of a chore chart or reward system may wear off quickly for children with ADD. Reward them immediately after they complete a chore and change the rewards frequently.

Use Alarms

An alarm, whether it's on your phone or it's a kitchen timer, can help you keep your day on track. An alarm helps you monitor your focus and productivity. When the alarm goes off, ask yourself, *What am I doing? Is this what I should be doing?* Just being aware of your behavior can create changes. You can set an alarm to remind yourself to take your medication or leave for an appointment. You can set a timer on your phone to remind yourself you have something cooking in the oven. If you must leave the kitchen, the alarm will still be with you.

People with ADD tend to get sucked into the television or computer. You tell yourself that you will watch just this one show or visit this one website, and before you know it, you have been sitting there for hours. Before you sit down to watch television or use the Internet, set a timer. When the timer goes off, turn off the television or log off of the Internet and leave the room. You can also set the auto-shutoff feature on your television or use auto-shutoff software on your laptop. It is recommended to use auto-shutoff because it can be a challenge to turn the television or computer off yourself.

Give Yourself a Head Start

An important part of being on time is to realize that getting there will probably take longer than you expected. You may be stuck in line somewhere before your next appointment, or you may get stuck in traffic. Schedule in some extra time to reduce your stress level and help you arrive on time.

While GPS has been very useful in helping people get from point A to point B, the GPS screen can be distracting, especially for people with ADD. Make sure you keep your eyes on the road and learn to use the auditory directions more than the visual ones. Remember to also print directions out ahead of time (these also will tell you the estimated time to reach your destination) and have regular maps in your car just in case your GPS points you in the wrong direction (or you go in the wrong direction).

The Phone Is for Your Convenience

Interruptions, such as a ringing phone, are much more startling and distracting to people with ADD. You may feel that you must answer the phone every time it rings. Your phone is there for your convenience, not the other way around. Put your phone on "silent" before you begin an activity. While many people have opted to get rid of their landline at their home, I recommend that you still retain a home phone. Remember, you still can call 911 if there is an emergency, even if your home phone doesn't have service. Home voice mail services allow you to have more than one in-box for incoming messages. You have one mailbox, your spouse has another, and your children have yet another. This way, you don't have to retrieve and deliver other people's messages, and you're less likely to lose someone's message.

STOP UNWANTED CALLS

It is a waste of your time and energy to have telemarketers call your home. The National Do Not Call Registry allows you to remove your phone numbers (both home and cell) from telemarketers' call lists. There is no fee for signing up. Avoid private companies that claim they can put your number on the registry for a fee. Telemarketers must stop calling you beginning thirty-one days after you put your numbers on the registry. The registry does not stop all telemarketers; political parties, charities, surveyors, and companies with which you already do business are exempt. Also avoid filling out any sweepstakes forms (either in person or online) that state in fine print that by submitting the form, you are allowing the company to contact you. Contact information for the National Do Not Call Registry can be found at the end of this chapter.

USE A HEADSET

When you balance the phone on your shoulder while you are doing another task, two things happen. First, you are putting a great deal of stress on your neck, and second, you are not effectively completing the task at hand. A phone headset, such as one that uses Bluetooth technology, allows you to talk on your phone hands free. You focus more on your task instead of the pain in your neck—or you can focus on the pain in the neck on the other end of the phone.

People with ADD shouldn't use their phone at all while driving—even with use of a headset or if your car is equipped with Bluetooth technology. Talking on the phone is just an added distraction. Remember, you are driving a two-and-a-half ton (2,000 kg) vehicle at a high rate of speed. Keep your eyes (and brain) on the road. And under no circumstance should someone be texting and driving, ADD or not.

CALL COMPANIES AT OPTIMUM TIMES

To get the best and fastest customer service, call companies at their off-peak hours, when there are fewer customer calls. It is best to call in the middle of the week during midmorning hours. By midmorning, employees have settled into their workday, and the rush of morning work has subsided. In addition, if you reach an automated system and really need to talk to a human, immediately pressing "0" may get you more quickly connected to a customer-service representative.

MAKE A LIST OF THINGS TO SAY

Phone calls are shorter and more effective if you have compiled a list of things to tell the person. If possible, postpone the call until you have a full list. Without a list, it is easy to get sidetracked and forget important items. A list will help you think more clearly, and the other person will be grateful to you for keeping the call short and to the point.

CONSIDER CONTACTING COMPANIES ONLINE INSTEAD

Using online customer service may cut down on the human element, but it may be quicker and more productive than calling the company directly. Plus, you are able to more easily keep records of your communication with the company if you use online chat or e-mail with a company representative.

Use E-Mail Productively

E-mail can be a productive and efficient way to communicate, or it can be a nightmare of overflowing messages and wasted time. Here are some ways to use e-mail to your advantage:

- Keep messages short enough that the recipient can see your entire message on one screen.

- If you don't need someone to respond to your e-mail, say so in your message.

- Keep questions in your e-mails to a yes-or-no format.

- If you receive an e-mail that asks you detailed questions, type your answers in a different font color directly after the original questions.

- Once you write an e-mail, it can be forwarded by the recipient to other people without your permission. Before sending a message, ask yourself if you would mind if other people read it.

- If you want to make sure someone received your e-mail, check your e-mail program for the "read receipt" option. This feature allows you to automatically receive an e-mail when the recipient has opened your e-mail.

- Unsubscribe from mass mailings you do not read. Usually, there is an "unsubscribe" link at the bottom of the e-mail.

- Schedule a time to answer your e-mail. Enforce a time limit on your e-mail use.

- If you receive an attachment you were not expecting, do not open it.

- Send yourself an e-mail to remind yourself of important information for the next day.

- E-mail yourself important documents in case your computer crashes or if you use more than one computer.

- Turn off the e-mail notification lights and sounds on your phone.

- If you have an issue with writing impulsive e-mails, use a service that has you wait or makes you complete a task before you can send out an e-mail.

Limit Your Use of Social Networking Sites

Using social networking sites can be fun but addictive, and this is especially true if you have ADD. Set a timer before you go on to a social networking site. When the timer goes off, log off from the site. If you are going to spend time on social networking sites, choose just one site to focus on. In addition, turn off phone and e-mail notifications from social networking sites.

Figure Out Your Most Productive Time

Some people are morning larks, while others are night owls. Your body clock is largely determined by genetics and hormones. Many people with ADD find that they are "wired" to stay up late and wake up late. To determine your most productive times of day, review your work schedule. When do you feel most alert? When do you feel tired? Schedule your most demanding tasks for the times of day when you are most productive. During times when you have less energy, schedule tasks that require less brain power.

Schedule E-Cards Ahead of Time

Sit down and schedule a bunch of e-cards to be sent throughout the year. Also, keep a few cards on hand for people who might not have e-mail. While sending a "real" card would be preferable, let's face it—sending out an e-card is better than sending nothing. An e-card saves time and energy, and it gets the job done. Keep in mind, however, that you should always send out real thank-you notes, as you will read more about in chapter 9.

Avoid Perfectionism

Sometimes, people with ADD can be so caught up in compensating for their difficulties focusing and following through that they get into the perfectionist zone. This is the feeling that you must do everything perfectly. You may remember times when you were penalized for careless errors. Remember, even people without ADD are not perfect. Give yourself a break, and allow yourself to relax. Set challenging yet achievable goals for yourself.

Schedule In Transition Time

When you have ADD, it can be difficult to make the transition from one setting to another. You may have difficulty transitioning from waking up in the morning to getting out the door to go to work. You may have difficulties shifting from getting ready for bed to actually going to sleep. You may have difficulties with transition times in the workplace.

To create a smoother transition from waking up in the morning to getting out the door, lay out your clothing the night before. Buy a coffeemaker that you can program to automatically turn on in the morning. You may want to wake up a half hour earlier just to have some more time to get ready. To make going to bed easier, play relaxing music from the time you start getting ready for bed until you go to sleep. Also practice a relaxation activity before bed. For more information on relaxation activities, see chapter 7.

When you arrive at work, shut the door to your office and spend the first half hour of your day reviewing your schedule for that day, returning a few of your less stressful calls or e-mails, and making a list of the people you need to talk to that day. When you arrive home after work, give yourself fifteen minutes to put away your briefcase and change into more comfortable clothes. In addition, set limits on answering work calls and e-mails after you get home. Try to leave your work at the office as much as possible.

Another important transition is getting back into work mode after being on vacation. Here are some tips:

- Plan for some downtime on Monday morning. Do not schedule any appointments. Just take time to go through the items that were left for you while you were away.

- Before you get back to work, have someone in the office organize your phone messages and memos into distinct piles.

- If you fly a long distance for a one-day business meeting, it may be worthwhile to arrive a day early. This will allow you to focus and prepare for your meeting. You also get to spend some time exploring the city, and you will not be as exhausted when you return.

Just Do It

Putting things off is very common among people with ADD. You want to do things that are fun and exciting, not dull and detailed. But sometimes, the dull and detailed stuff just has to get done. It is best to get the boring stuff over with first. If you really want to put something off, ask yourself, If I don't do this now, when will I do it? Usually, the best time is now.

Exercise: Create a Weekly Schedule

When people with ADD lack structure or a set schedule in their day, they can feel unproductive and frustrated. When people with ADD know what to expect, they are more focused and productive. A structured schedule does not mean a rigid schedule. If your spouse or partner asks you out to dinner on a weeknight, don't say, "I'm sorry, that is not on my weekly schedule." Just go.

Create a schedule of your week. There are spreadsheet programs and smartphone calendar apps that can streamline the schedule creating process.

1. Create a calendar where each day of the week is divided into half-hour increments (9:00, 9:30, 10:00). Start with the time you usually wake up and end with the time you usually go to bed.

2. For every half hour, write down what you plan on doing at that time. Make sure every half-hour slot is filled up. Remember to include the time you spend

   • commuting

   • eating breakfast, lunch, and dinner

- spending free time
- studying
- working
- socializing

3. Designate a color for each activity. For example, make "studying time" blue and "working time" red. People with ADD are very visual, so it will be much easier for you to just glance at the color on your schedule rather than read the name of the activity.

When you have ADD, it is easy to over-focus on one area to the detriment of others. Make sure you have a balance between the time you spend on work, social activities, and family activities. It is important to include time for relaxing and rejuvenating. You may relax by reading a book or by going out with friends—it all depends on your personal style.

If you use a paper planner, print out your schedule, hole-punch it, and put it in your planner. If you're using a smartphone app, make sure you back up your schedule onto a hard drive and an online calendar app.

Time management is possible for people with ADD. It may take a little while to adapt to new time management behaviors, but the reduction in your stress level and the positive response from family and friends will be worth your effort. In the next chapter, you will learn ADD-friendly techniques for money management.

Resources

Morgenstern, J. 2004. *Time Management from the Inside Out: The Foolproof System for Taking Control of Your Schedule— and Your Life*. 2nd ed. New York: Holt Paperbacks.

Ratey, N. 2008. *The Disorganized Mind: Coaching Your ADHD Brain to Take Control of Your Time, Tasks, and Talents*. New York: St. Martin's Griffin.

ADD Consults
www.addconsults.com

ADHD Coaches Organization
www.adhdcoaches.org

American Coaching Association
www.americoach.org
2141 Birch Drive
Lafayette Hill, PA 19444
Tel: (610) 825-8572
Fax: (610) 825-4505

CNET
www.cnet.com

Consumer Reports
www.consumerreports.org

Dragon speech recognition software
www.nuance.com/dragon/index.htm

National Do Not Call Registry
www.donotcall.gov
(888) 382-1222

Make Your Money Work for You

People with ADD have a peculiar form of long-term financial blindness. They usually cannot look into the future and see that they will eventually retire. Financial planning does not come easily to people with ADD, and the usual recommendations include detailed, boring work, such as establishing a budget. Even when people with ADD are able to establish a budget, they have great difficulty following it. To achieve financial success, people with ADD may need to rely on nontraditional methods of financial management.

You may have some of the following problems regarding your finances:

- late fees on bills because you forgot to pay them

- bounced checks

- difficulties saving money

- a checkbook that isn't balanced

- impulsive buying

- credit card debt

- putting off paying taxes

- losing important financial documents

When you consider how much money you have lost due to late fees, bounced checks, and debt, it can get pretty depressing. People with ADD have more debt and money-related stress than people without ADD. In this chapter, you will learn ways to manage your finances confidently and effectively.

The Grocery Shopping Jungle

According to a study by Kaufman-Scarborough and Cohen (2004), 92 percent of people with ADD reported impulsive shopping, and almost 62 percent routinely left the store without buying needed items. For the person with ADD, a trip to the grocery store can feel like a jungle adventure. You forget your coupons, there are too many items to choose from, and the noise can be aggravating. Here are some tips for getting through the grocery shopping jungle.

DON'T GO TO THE GROCERY STORE HUNGRY

You are more likely to buy items on impulse when you grocery shop on an empty stomach. Keep some snacks in your car in case you need something to eat before you shop.

ALWAYS GO TO THE STORE
WITH A LIST

Make a list of the items you usually buy at the grocery store. Photocopy this list, laminate it, and keep it on your refrigerator. When you need an item, circle it on the list with a dry-erase marker. When your food supply is getting low, go to the grocery store with your list. Try to buy only what is on your list. Once you're done shopping, wipe off the list and post it back on the fridge. You can also get a grocery list app for your smartphone.

People with ADD are creative and inspired, and you may see something in the store that catches your eye. It's okay to try something new (in moderation), but don't forget to buy the bread and milk also.

GO GROCERY SHOPPING
WITH SOMEONE

You are more likely to buy the items on your list and *only* the items on your list if you go with a friend or family member to the store. Preferably, the person you are going with is a smart shopper and is not prone to impulsive purchases.

LOOK FOR STORE BRANDS

Stores display the most expensive brands at eye level. Look below for lower-priced store-brand items. Often, the quality is just as good, and the product may even be manufactured in the same plant. Also, note that the items positioned on the end of the aisles are not always on sale.

CHECK YOUR CART

Before entering the checkout line, review the items in your cart. Determine which items you really need and which you picked out on impulse. Put back any impulse items you don't really want. Make sure you bought everything on your list.

ONLINE SHOPPING

While you shop online, time can fly by. Set a timer as you begin, and when the timer goes off, you are done. Turn off "1-click" ordering on websites. This feature separates you from your money before you have time to think about your purchase. In addition, for online shopping safety, use a prepaid credit card that isn't linked to your bank accounts. For links to online discounts, see the resources section at the end of this chapter.

Be a Smart Consumer

While groceries can certainly add up, it's even more important to shop wisely when you're making larger purchases.

RESEARCH BEFORE YOU PURCHASE

Research the quality of an item by reading consumer magazines or websites. Sometimes the cheaper brand is just as good as—if not better than—the expensive brand. Sometimes you find through research that the more costly brand is the best. A list of consumer publications and websites can be found at the end of this chapter.

SKIP REBATES

Don't buy something just because there is a rebate attached. Forty percent of rebates never get redeemed, either because people send in the wrong paperwork or don't send in the rebate at all (Grow 2005). In addition, studies show that the longer you wait after a purchase, the less likely you will send in rebate forms (Silk 2004).

DON'T TOUCH ANYTHING AT THE STORE

When you touch an item on a store shelf, you are much more prone to buying it (Wolf, Arkes, and Muhanna 2008). This is one of the reasons why retailers encourage you to "try before you buy." Once you have physical contact with the item, you are much more likely to claim it as yours. So avoid any try-before-you-buy deals, and keep your hands off that store shelf!

DETERMINE THE COST PER USE

Be aware of an item's cost per use. It may be worth it in the long run to buy a more expensive product. For example, suppose you're shopping for a new printer, and you estimate that you print 1,000 pages per year. If a printer costs $100 and uses ink cartridges that cost $20 and last for about 250 pages, each page you print in the first year would cost you 18 cents. Over time, it might actually cost less to buy a more expensive printer if it uses cheaper cartridges or the cartridges last significantly longer.

REVIEW YOUR PURCHASE WITH SOMEONE ELSE

Make a rule that before you buy an item that costs over $100, you will go home and consult with a family member or friend about the purchase. This helps keep your impulse shopping in check.

Avoid Extended Warranties

When you buy items, particularly electronics, you may be offered an extended warranty or service contract. Don't buy it. According to *Consumer Reports* (2005), many items are very unlikely to break in the first three years.

CARE FOR YOUR BELONGINGS

Items can break, become unsafe, and lose their value if you do not maintain them. Your car is one of your most valuable possessions. Make sure you have the suggested maintenance done, or you may wind up paying more in the long run for repairs.

Invest in Money Management Software

Money management software, such as Quicken or Microsoft Money, can help you by

- balancing your checking accounts

- organizing your investments and updating their value daily

- reminding you when bills are due

- automatically paying bills online

- creating graphs of your spending and saving habits

- providing a list of your tax deductible expenses

- filing your taxes online

For the money management software to download your credit card statements, bank statements, or investments, your bank or investment group must have online banking services that are compatible with your money management software.

You will be more successful in sticking with the software if you have someone teach you how to use it.

Money management software takes a lot of the monotony and tediousness out of money management. Once you get into the habit of using the software, you will be able to keep more money in the bank. You will no longer lose money because of late fees or bounced checks. You'll also have less stress since the software reminds you to pay your bills or will do it automatically for you. You may even realize that you had more money than you thought—and wind up with more money than you ever imagined.

Shop Around for a Bank or Credit Union

You have more power than ever to choose a bank or credit union that meets your needs and costs you the least. You may be familiar with banks but not as familiar with credit unions. Credit unions are not for profit and are owned by their account holders. Both banks and credit unions are regulated by the federal government. When looking for a bank, ask the following questions:

- Does the bank charge a fee if you go below a certain balance in your account?

- Does the bank charge a fee if you write over a certain number of checks a month?

- Does the bank charge a fee for using ATMs?

- Does the bank have competitive interest rates?

- Are the bank's online services compatible with your money management software?

- Does the bank have locations that are close to your home or office?

You can also shop around online for the best interest rates on loans and credit cards. See the resources at the end of this chapter for more information.

Do not buy checks from your bank. It is much cheaper to buy checks through a printing company. Do you really need two boxes of checks? You should be paying all of your bills electronically; therefore, you will be using fewer of those checks as time goes on. When you do buy checks, choose checks with carbons. A carbon sheet directly underneath each check makes a copy so you will know exactly whom you wrote the check to and for how much. Checks with carbons are more expensive, but they are definitely worth it. You can also print out checks from your computer if you have money management software.

Simplify Your Money

The best way to manage your money is to make it as simple as possible. Here are some suggestions.

HIRE SOMEONE TO DO YOUR TAXES

Taxes are tedious and detailed, making them especially challenging for people with ADD. You may think you can't afford to hire someone to do your taxes. However, it costs you more money if you make careless errors or if you don't mail your taxes in on time. One exception to this is if you have very few accounts or investments, no dependents, and only work for one employer. If that is the case, you might want to consider using tax software that syncs with your money management software. You can find more information about this at the end of this chapter.

USE DIRECT DEPOSIT

Many businesses now electronically deposit paychecks into employees' accounts. This means you no longer have to wait in line at the bank, and some banks even waive fees if you have direct deposit. Direct deposit helps you save money since you can't cash your paycheck and spend it all. Ask your employer if they participate in direct deposit.

HAVE AN EMERGENCY FUND

Automatically deposit a portion of your paycheck into savings each month. Aim to have an emergency fund in your savings account equal to about two months' income. This money provides a cushion in case there is a sudden job loss or a death in the family. Put your emergency fund in an account with easy access so you can retrieve the money as soon as you need it.

USE AUTOMATIC PAYMENT

When you set up automatic payments, you authorize companies to take money out of your account to pay your bills. This means that you do not have to write a check every month. When setting up automatic payments, you can ask companies to reschedule your bill due dates so they all fall on the same day. If you receive two paychecks a month, you can schedule your bill due dates in two batches, one after each payday. Scheduling your bill due dates streamlines your bill-paying process.

There are drawbacks to automatic payment. If you have a dispute over a bill, the payment has already been taken out of your account. Also, you must make sure you have enough money in your account at the time of the automatic with-drawal. Being overdrawn can add up to costly bank charges. It can be easy to forget when the money is due when you are not writing a check every month.

CARRY A LIMITED AMOUNT OF CASH

Determine the total amount of cash you really need every week. Withdraw only this much cash. When you run out of cash, you are done spending until the following week.

Limit your usage of ATMs. When you use an ATM, you get cash quickly—not a good idea for a person with ADD. The more cash you have with you, the more you are likely to spend. If you do use ATMs, choose a bank that does not charge a fee. One or two dollars for each ATM withdrawal may not seem like a lot, but it adds up quickly. Also beware of getting cash back from a debit card purchase at a store. Taking that extra cash out can add up.

USE A BILL-PAYING BASKET

It is recommended that you pay all your bills online and receive statements via e-mail rather than paper. However, if a company does not have an online payment option, there is a way to keep track of your paper bills and statements. Keep all of your bill-paying supplies in a basket. Fill the basket with some envelopes, stamps, your checkbook, and a pen. When a bill arrives, bring it to the bill-paying basket, and write a check right then and there.

KEEP TRACK OF RECEIPTS

Receipts seem to multiply when you are not looking. Only keep receipts you may need in the future:

- receipts for major purchases
- receipts for business purchases

- receipts for items you may need to return

- receipts for tax deductible expenses and donations

- receipts for expenses for which you will be reimbursed

Buy a check-size accordion folder with pockets for each month. When you get a receipt, file it under that month. Make sure you file your receipts immediately. At the end of the year, go through the receipts and discard any you no longer need. Save receipts for tax deductible expenses separately in an envelope marked "(Year) Tax Receipts."

The Internal Revenue Service (IRS) does not require a receipt for anything under $75. Some financial professionals may recommend that you keep these receipts. However, if you have ADD and are prone to clutter, it may be better to toss these receipts after you have recorded the amount for your taxes.

USE A RECEIPT SCANNER

Not only can a receipt scanner keep track of your receipts, some can also scan business cards and automatically collect all of the information from the business card—name, address, and contact numbers. You can then put this information into your computer's contact information software, such as Outlook. Some receipts are printed on thermal paper (paper that feels slick to the touch). Make sure you scan these receipts first, as the printing on them can fade quickly. The IRS accepts electronic scans of receipts for tax purposes. More information on receipt scanners can be found in the resources section at the end of this book.

ADD and Debt

People with ADD have a higher rate of debt (Barkley, Murphy, and Fischer 2008). This is due, in part, to impulsive spending and disorganization. How many times have you bought something only to realize you already had one just like it? These costs can add up.

FIND AFFORDABLE HEALTH INSURANCE

Health insurance can be expensive. However, because people with ADD have higher medical costs, higher prescription costs, and a higher rate of injuries and accidents than people without ADD, it is very important to have health care coverage (Kleinman et al. 2009; Sabuncuoglu 2007; Secnik, Swensen, and Lage 2005). If your employer doesn't offer health insurance and an individual plan is too expensive, check into federal, state, or local health insurance programs.

REDUCE CREDIT CARD USE

Many money management books will tell you to completely stop using your credit cards. However, cutting off credit cards completely not only is unrealistic for people with ADD, it can also lead to binge use of the credit cards. It is human nature that the more something is prohibited, the more you want to do it. This is especially true in people with ADD.

Instead of going cold turkey, work to become more aware of your credit card use. Using credit cards responsibly helps your credit rating and saves you money. You will learn more about your credit rating later in this chapter. The Credit Card Accountability, Responsibility, and Disclosure (CARD) Act of

2009 created more protection for credit card users, but you should still pay attention to the details in your credit card agreement and any agreement updates you receive from your card issuer.

Consider getting a prepaid credit card. This is a credit card on which you put a set amount of money, and it is not linked to your bank accounts. This type of card not only helps reduce impulsive spending but also helps protect you from identity theft.

To avoid problems with credit cards, pay cash whenever possible. You can also pay using a debit card. If you do so, make sure your purchases are recorded in your money management software or checkbook so you can avoid overdrawing your account.

It is important to work on paying off your credit cards. When you purchase an item with a credit card, you have taken out a loan at an extremely high interest rate. Write down the interest rates and balances of all your credit cards. Pay off the card with the highest interest rate first. When that card is paid off, work on the card with the next highest interest rate.

PAY YOUR CREDITORS

Do you have accounts that have been turned over to a collection agency? Here are some tips.

Set Up a Payment Plan

Call the creditor and arrange to pay a certain amount of your bill each month. Creditors are much more understanding if you make an effort to pay them instead of ignoring your debt.

Know Your Rights

The Fair Debt Collection Practices Act provides you with certain rights. While the act does not forgive your debt, it creates boundaries to protect you.

- A collection agency can call you only between 8:00 a.m. and 9:00 p.m. in your time zone.

- A collection agency cannot contact anyone else about your debt except your attorney if you have one. They are allowed to call people to get your address and phone number, but they may not discuss your debt or identify themselves as a collection agency unless specifically asked.

- You can stop a collection agency from calling you by writing a letter to the agency within thirty days of their first contact. The letter must state that you do not want the collection agency to contact you. It would be best to send this letter via certified mail.

- A collection agency cannot threaten you with jail, use obscene language, use a false name, deposit a postdated check before the date written, make you accept collect calls, or collect any amount of money greater than the actual debt (unless allowed by law).

- If you feel your rights have been violated, you can report the violation to the Federal Trade Commission. For contact information, see the end of this chapter. You can also file a federal or state lawsuit against the debt collector. You usually have to file a lawsuit within one year of the collection agency's first contact with you.

CHECK YOUR CREDIT REPORT

Your *credit report* contains information about your credit accounts (credit cards, loans, and debts), their balances, and the promptness of your payments. This information is collected and sold by companies called *credit bureaus*. You are given a credit rating based on the information in your credit report. The better your credit report, the higher your credit rating. Your *credit rating* and report can influence your chances of getting credit cards, a mortgage, and loans.

Obtain a copy of your credit report from each of the three credit bureaus: Experian, Equifax, and TransUnion. Review the reports for accuracy, especially if you are planning to apply for a credit card or loan in the near future. Credit reports can cost up to $9 or they can be free, depending on where you live, your employment status, and whether you have been turned down for a credit card or loan in the past sixty days. Contact the credit bureaus immediately if you find inaccurate information on your credit report. Contact information for the credit bureaus can be found at the end of this chapter.

Be Cautious with Your Social Security Number

Identity theft, where someone steals your name, Social Security number, or other identifying information, is on the rise. From 2003 to 2006, the rate of identity-theft victims increased 50 percent. During this time period, fifteen million people in the United States experienced someone stealing their identity (Soat 2007).

The thief who steals your identity can then use your credit cards, apply for loans in your name, and cause other financial nightmares. When destroying documents that contain your Social Security number or other identifying information, use a crosscut shredder. If someone has stolen your identity, contact the credit bureaus listed at the end of this chapter.

Develop a Budget

Although creating a detailed budget may not be possible, you need to look at your major monthly expenses. Budget planning can be done in a notebook, with a budget workbook, or with financial software. First, write down your nonnegotiable payments. For example, your mortgage or rent and your car payment are fixed, obligatory monthly amounts. Then write down your immediate necessities, such as food, electricity, and medication. Finally, write down the discretionary items on your budget, like entertainment, eating out, and gifts for family and friends.

Next, write down your monthly income. Subtract your total expenses from your monthly income. Do you have money left at the end of the month? Remember, in the words of Suze Orman, "It's not what you make—it's what you get to keep" (1997, 125).

If you are spending more than you are bringing in, look at how much you have spent over the last few months. Are there any areas where you could spend less? For example, while food is a necessity, you have some control over the total monthly cost. You may need to buy less-expensive food.

Also look at the little ways you spend money. For example, if you buy one gourmet coffee drink every week at $4, in a year you will spend $208. Imagine how it adds up if you buy one every day. You do not have to detail every purchase down to the penny. You will always have some small purchases that will be difficult to track and include in your budget. Researching these items is not worth the time and aggravation. You are looking for an approximate budget. You can find a budget-creation exercise at the end of this chapter.

Take Advantage of Tax-Free Savings

People with ADD often have difficulty saving for future needs. Let's take a look at two smart ways to save your money.

INVEST IN A TAX-FREE RETIREMENT ACCOUNT

You may qualify for an *individual retirement account* (IRA). An IRA allows you to deposit up to a certain amount of income every year. The earnings are tax deferred until withdrawals are made. Some employers offer a 401(k) retirement plan. If you enroll, your employer may match the 401(k) funds you have contributed to your account.

START A PREPAID COLLEGE TUITION FUND

A *529 plan* allows you to deposit money in an account every month for your child's college tuition—tax free. See the resources at the end of this chapter for more information.

Set Financial Goals

By establishing immediate, short-term, and long-term financial goals, you are defining what you would like to accomplish. You are more likely to control your spending if you have financial goals.

Financial management is possible when you have ADD. You just need a less detail-intensive way of doing it. In the next chapter, you will learn how taking care of yourself can reduce some ADD symptoms.

Exercise: Create a Budget

Use the following worksheet to determine your monthly budget. You don't need to get the dollar amounts down to the penny. Just writing a dollar amount is fine. First write down your monthly income. Because many people with ADD have difficulties with math, here are some formulas for figuring out your monthly income:

- Weekly pay times four

- Bi-monthly pay times two

- If your income varies widely from month to month, find out the yearly total and divide by twelve.

Now fill in your fixed and flexible expenses. If you pay your car insurance every six months, divide that payment by six to get your monthly payment. Remember that this budget is just a guideline. Feel free to add or delete items as you see fit.

Income:

Work _____

Other Income _____

Total _____

Fixed Expenses:

Car Payment _____

Rent _____

Cable _____

Internet _____

Electricity _____

Telephone _____

Tuition _____

Car Insurance _____

Health Insurance _____

Medications _____

Fuel/Gas _____

Child Support _____

Alimony _____

Savings _____

Total _____

Flexible Expenses:

Eating Out _____

Snacks _____

Vacation/Trips _____

Concerts/Music _____

Game tickets _____

Groceries _____

Clothing _____

Gifts _____

Hobbies _____

Total _____

Total of Fixed +
Flexible Expenses _____

Income – Expenses _____

Your main goal is to have money left over after you subtract your expenses from your income. Even if that number is just $20 or $30, you are still on the right track.

Exercise: Discover Your Financial Goals

I.   Grab a pen and a piece of paper.

• At the top of one of the sheets, write "Immediate Goals."

- On another sheet, write "Short-Term Goals."

- On the third sheet, write "Long-Term Goals."

2. Start with the "Immediate Goals" paper. These are money goals you would like to accomplish within a month. You can write as many as you want. Be realistic about your goals. For example, you might not want to write "Own a yacht" on the "Immediate Goals" list unless you are independently wealthy. Items for your "Immediate Goals" list might include

- Learn how to use money management software.

- Work on my money management once a week.

- Make car payment on time this month.

- Make a list of when my bills are due.

3. On your "Short-Term Goals" list, write down money goals you would like to accomplish within one year. Items for this list might include

- Pay off two of my credit cards.

- Get a better interest rate on my car loan.

- Send off my taxes on time.

- Put away money in my savings account every month.

4. Long-term goals are those you would like to accomplish within five years. This list might include

  - Pay off all credit cards.

  - Have the equivalent of six months' salary in my savings account.

  - Buy a new car.

  - Get a new roof for the house.

You have something to aim for when you create goals for yourself. Look at your lists and update them as you achieve your goals. When you get frustrated, take out your goals and review them. Remind yourself why you are working at organizing your money: so your money can work for you.

Resources

Sarkis, S., and K. Klein. 2009. *ADD and Your Money: A Guide to Personal Finance for Adults with Attention Deficit Disorder.* Oakland, CA: New Harbinger Publications, Inc.

Tyson, E. 2009. *Personal Finance for Dummies,* 6th ed. Hoboken, NJ: Wiley Publishing Inc.

CREDIT BUREAUS

Equifax
www.equifax.com
(800) 685-1111

Experian
www.experian.com
(888) 397-3742

TransUnion
www.transunion.com
(800) 888-4213

REPORTING IDENTITY THEFT

Equifax
(800) 525-6285

Experian
(888) 397-3742

TransUnion
(800) 680-7289

Federal Trade Commission identity theft website
www.consumer.gov/idtheft/index.html
(877) 438-4338

MONEY MANAGEMENT

529 Plans
www.savingforcollege.com

Consumer Advocate
www.clarkhoward.com

Team Clark consumer phone bank
(404) 892-8227

Consumer Reports
www.consumerreports.org
Subscription department: (800) 208-9696

Credit Card Information
www.creditcards.com

Credit Union National Association
www.creditunion.coop/

Federal Trade Commission
www.ftc.gov
(877) 382-4357

Interest Rates
www.bankrate.com

RetailMeNot
www.retailmenot.com

Turbo Tax
http://turbotax.intuit.com/

7

Practice Good Self-Care

In chapter 6, you learned about managing money. Financial wellness is an important part of your life. However, there are other kinds of wellness that are equally important. In this chapter, you will learn about the different dimensions of wellness and how to have a more balanced life.

Because people with ADD live fairly fast-paced lives, they can forget to slow down a little and consider whether they are living a balanced life. When you are on an airplane, you are told by the flight attendant that you must put on your oxygen mask before you put on your child's. This is similar to everyday life. You can't take care of others unless you take care of yourself first. Make time every day to maintain your body, spirit, and intellect. If you need help finding the time for wellness, refer to chapter 5, "Manage Your Time."

Use the Wellness Model

Practicing wellness means making changes to ensure that you have balance in your life. There are six dimensions to wellness: physical, social, occupational, spiritual, intellectual, and emotional.

The physical dimension is the ability to exercise, eat healthy foods, get proper medical care, abstain from addictive substances, and practice stress reduction and relaxation. The social dimension is the ability to interact with a variety of people, communicate effectively, enrich your community, develop friendships, have fun, and balance work and play. You will learn more about social wellness in chapters 9 and 10.

The occupational dimension is the ability to enjoy your work, search for jobs, and find a job that is suited to your skills and needs. It is also the ability to recognize opportunities for learning new skills. You will learn more about occupational wellness in chapter 8. The spiritual dimension is the ability to participate in spiritual activities, protect the environment, define your ethics and purpose in life, and care about the welfare of others.

The intellectual dimension is the ability to follow current events, experience new things, observe your environment, and use critical thinking skills. It is also the ability to solve problems. The emotional dimension is the ability to express emotions, control emotions, learn effective and healthy coping skills, view life positively, and maintain independence while knowing when you need help from others. It is also the ability to create realistic goals for yourself.

People with ADD tend to be overzealous in a particular area of wellness. They can ignore other areas of wellness for extended periods of time. This imbalance can lead you to feel off-kilter, unhappy, and depressed. In this chapter, you will learn ADD-specific strategies for keeping your dimensions of wellness balanced. In chapter 8, you will learn about occupational well-being. In chapter 9, you will learn about social well-being. In this chapter, you will learn how to improve your physical, emotional, and spiritual dimensions of wellness.

Achieve Physical Wellness

Your physical well-being is largely determined by exercise, diet, and sleep habits.

START EXERCISING

What if you were told that there was an inexpensive, healthy, and fun way to reduce the severity of your ADD symptoms? There is: physical exercise. Exercise also helps reduce depression and anxiety, which people with ADD experience at a higher rate (Kiluk, Weden, and Culotta 2009; Secnik, Swensen, and Lage 2005). As you read in chapter 1, people with ADD have a low level of the brain chemical dopamine. Exercising can raise your dopamine level, thereby improving your ability to focus. It is best to exercise first thing in the morning so you feel the benefits of this dopamine boost for the rest of the day. Just thirty minutes a day, three times a week can help you feel better.

Exercising does not need to cost a lot of money. If you have exercise shoes, you already have the necessary equipment. If you are just starting to exercise, take it slowly. Do not over-exert yourself. You can cause injuries if you push yourself too hard. Talk to your doctor before starting an exercise program. Exercising is like learning how to drive a manual transmission car. At first it can be tough, but after awhile you don't even think about it—you just do it.

You can keep track of your exercise habits by either writing down your activities in a notebook or by using an app that keeps track of it for you. Knowing that you are keeping a record of your exercising makes it more likely you will continue to be active. For information on exercise apps, see the end of this chapter.

Find an Exercise Partner

Finding an exercise partner greatly increases your chances of staying with an exercise program. Knowing that someone is meeting you to exercise gives you more motivation—you are now accountable to another person. See the end of this chapter for information on websites that can help you find an exercise partner.

Many people have a canine exercise partner. Dogs love going for walks, and they can usually keep up with you. An added bonus is that a canine exercise partner is almost always available.

Vary Your Exercise Routine

To a person with ADD, variety is truly the spice of life. To combat exercise boredom, vary your routine. Walk around your neighborhood, take a group exercise class, take a lunchtime walk with your coworkers, or work in your garden. If you weigh 150 pounds, you burn as many calories during sixty minutes of gardening as you do jogging for forty-five minutes. The activity is not as important as the fact that you are being active.

Find the Time to Exercise

You do have time to exercise. It all depends on whether you make exercise a priority. If you have difficulties getting up in the morning, exercise in the evening. If you are exhausted after work, exercise first thing in the morning. For help fitting exercise into your schedule, see chapter 5.

EAT WELL

The best way to maintain a healthy body is to combine exercise with eating well.

Having ADD can make it easier to put weight on and harder to take the weight off (Davis et al. 2006; Altfas 2002). Staying focused on a weight loss program can be difficult for people with ADD. It is especially tedious when it takes awhile for the weight to come off. People with ADD like immediate gratification, and achieving a healthy body weight takes time. Here are some realistic ways to eat well.

Beware of Fad Diets

Before starting any diet, check with your doctor. Keep in mind that women with ADD are four times more likely to have an eating disorder, such as bulimia and anorexia, than non-ADD women (Biederman et al. 2007). Be cautious about fad diets. Fad diets promise quick weight loss and may promote unhealthy eating habits. Another caution about fad diets is that you quickly gain the weight back after you stop the diet. Fad diets are temporary. Changing your lifestyle and eating habits is a much better way to maintain your ideal weight.

Practice Portion Control

Portion control means that you don't eat an entire box of cookies at one sitting, even if they are low-fat cookies. Portion control means eating smaller amounts of food. Restaurants, particularly those in the United States, serve much larger portions than you actually need. You can always take home what you do not eat.

Keep track of what you are eating. You can either write down your food intake in a notebook or use an app to keep track of food amounts and calories. When you write down how much food you are consuming, it can be a real eye-opener. You may also find that writing down what you're eating causes you to eat more appropriate amounts of food. For information on exercise apps, see the end of this chapter.

Use a smaller plate when serving yourself at home or at a party. Before going to a party, eat something light. You will be less likely to gorge on party food later.

Eat Thoughtfully

It is easy to overeat when you are paying attention to something else. Focus on your food. People with ADD eat too quickly, which leads to overeating. ADD is not only a problem with focusing on the external environment; it is also a problem with focusing on the internal environment—your body. People with ADD have difficulties knowing when they are full. A solution is to practice mindful eating. When you are eating, chew slowly and focus on the taste of your food. Make a concerted effort to stay in the present moment.

Here are other ways to practice mindful eating.

- Do a blessing before dinner.

- Before you eat, look at the food and think about where it came from and the effort it took to bring it to your table.

- When you eat, do nothing else. Do not read or watch TV while you eat.

- Always sit down to eat. Do not eat standing up, on the run, or in your car.

- Take time to prepare your food. Do not eat it directly out of the box.

- Eat only foods that you truly enjoy.

When you practice mindful eating, you will notice that you need less food, and you will enjoy your food more. Eating will become a whole new experience for you.

When Eating Fast Food, Make Wise Choices

It is best to prepare a healthy meal before going on the road, but this is not always possible. However, you can make healthy choices at fast-food establishments. Avoid heavy sauces, fried foods, and sugary drinks. If you order a salad, choose low-fat dressing. Look for the restaurant's list of healthy menu items online or on the menu.

PRACTICE GOOD SLEEP HYGIENE

People with ADD have difficulties with sleeping and are more likely to have sleep disorders. They may have had impaired sleep since childhood (Gruber et al. 2008). People with ADD tend to have more problems with insomnia, obstructive sleep apnea, snoring, and restless leg syndrome (Walters et al. 2008; Wagner, Walters, and Fisher 2004). They are also more apt to have more difficulties falling asleep, wake up not feeling refreshed, and have a delayed onset of a brain chemical called *melatonin,* which regulates the body's sleep-wake cycle (Van Veen et al. 2010; Schredl, Alm, and Sobanski 2007). Sleep disorders may be caused by your environment, your genetics, or poor sleep hygiene. Sleep hygiene practices are healthy techniques for getting a good night's rest.

Use Transition Time

To make a smoother transition at bedtime, turn off the television or computer at least thirty minutes before you go to bed. The sensory stimulation and light emitting from electronic devices keeps your brain awake (Milian 2010). It is difficult for your brain to come down from all that stimulation. Spend the thirty minutes before bed engaging in a slower-paced activity, such as listening to relaxing music or petting your cat or dog. Set an alarm for thirty minutes before your bedtime to remind you to turn off the television or computer. You can also use the auto-shutoff feature on your television or auto-shutoff software on your computer. Having automatic shutoff is preferred because it can be difficult to motivate yourself to actually turn off electronics on your own. If you have children, turn off the television or computer even earlier—thirty minutes before your children go to bed. Once they are in bed, keep the television and computer off. Do a relaxing activity instead.

Keep a Consistent Bedtime

Go to bed at the same time every night, and get up at the same time every morning, regardless of the day of the week. On a workday, you may get up at 7:00 a.m. and go to bed at 11:00 p.m. On weekends, you may get up at 11:00 a.m. and go to bed at 2:00 a.m. Your body will have difficulty readjusting when Monday morning rolls around. Getting up every day at the same time helps your body regulate itself.

Use Your Bed for Only Two Activities

Use your bed only for sleeping and sex. Do not watch television, read, or do paperwork in your bedroom. It can hinder your sleep and cause distance between you and your spouse. Find another quiet location at home for these activities.

The more strongly you associate your bed with sleeping, the easier it will be for you to fall asleep.

Prevent Nighttime Teeth Grinding

If you have ADD, you may be prone to grinding your teeth at night while you sleep. This may be because you have excess energy that you are burning off at night. Grinding your teeth is called *bruxism*. If bruxism goes unchecked, it can lead to broken, worn, or sensitive teeth. It can also result in jaw muscle pain and headaches. A solution to bruxism is a *nightguard*, which protects your teeth from grinding together while you sleep. The nightguard is made out of acrylic material and is fitted to the shape of your teeth and bite. Not only will nightguards extend the life of your teeth, they will also help your spouse get a better night's rest. He or she will no longer have to listen to the sound of gnashing teeth. Ask your dentist about being fitted for a nightguard. There are less expensive nightguards available at drugstores, but keep in mind that they are not as effective as an acrylic nightguard available at your dentist's office.

LISTEN TO YOUR BODY

People with ADD not only have difficulties paying attention to the outside world, they also have difficulties paying attention to their inside world. You may go too long without eating because you do not sense that you are hungry. You may also overeat because you do not notice that you are full. You may go too long without sleep because you are too busy to notice your fatigue.

Check in with yourself during the day and ask, What is my body telling me? Think about how your body reacts in different situations: fatigue, hunger, sadness, boredom, and stress.

For example, when you are hungry, your stomach may growl or you may feel lightheaded. Your hands may become shaky. When you are more aware of how your body reacts, you can take steps to prevent wearing yourself out. For example, if you notice that you become ravenously hungry if you do not eat for six hours, make sure you eat every four hours.

It's important to check in with your doctor if you're not feeling well, especially if you are taking medications, have started a new medication, or if the dose was recently changed. Don't worry about "bothering" your doctor—he or she wants to know when your health is compromised. It's better to let him know now rather than wait until it becomes a crisis.

Achieve Emotional Wellness

Emotional wellness encompasses relaxation, positive attitude, creativity, and fun. Coping with your emotions is an important part of overall wellness.

LIMIT TELEVISION VIEWING

Researchers found that during prime time television, 80 percent of children's programs, 82 percent of drama programs, and 46 percent of reality programs contained violence (Smith, Nathanson, and Wilson 2002). Watching violence on television desensitizes people. The more violence you see on television, the less you are bothered by it, and you may become aggressive (Huesmann and Taylor 2006). Watching violence on TV actually changes your brain function, whether you have an aggressive personality or not (Mathews et al. 2005). When you see something horrific happening on the television news, you cannot help the victims. This can lead you to feel traumatized

(Schlenger et al. 2002). Also, watching the news on television can give you an exaggerated perception of the amount of crime in your area. Repeatedly watching a traumatic event on the news can make you feel helpless. Limit your television viewing and notice the change in your attitude—you may feel calmer and more optimistic.

REMEMBER TO HAVE FUN

Taking the seventh day to rest may be a religious concept, but it is grounded in good healthy living. This guideline is especially beneficial to people with ADD. Because of poor time management, people with ADD get more and more tired during the week. Remember, it is just as important to have fun and stay creative as it is to work. Pick a day each week to relax and have fun. If finding a day for rest seems daunting, see chapter 5, "Manage Your Time."

FIND A RELAXING ACTIVITY

While some people find meditation helpful in reducing stress, it can be difficult to sit and totally empty your mind if you have ADD. A relaxation activity that involves movement may be easier and more beneficial to you. For example, yoga involves stretching, deep breathing, and forming different postures. When you do yoga, you get the benefits of a relaxation activity combined with the movement that people with ADD need and crave.

Creative visualization is a good relaxation technique for people with ADD because it lets you use your imagination. It also keeps your mind active while you relax. There are CDs and tapes available that walk you through guided imagery. A narrator describes a scene, and your imagination follows.

REDUCE YOUR LEVEL OF ANGER

People with ADD can have a very short fuse—their anger can go from zero to sixty in a few seconds. Things that would not bother people without ADD can set you off. A common problem for people with ADD is that while they get over their outbursts rather quickly, family members may be traumatized for a long time. Angry outbursts can strain your relationships, leading to a damaging cycle of anger.

Anger is a normal human emotion. What matters is how you deal with your anger. You might think that when you yell, you are getting your point across more effectively. In reality, the more you yell, the less the other person listens to you. Anger is paradoxical. The more you try to eliminate your anger, the more it shows up. The goal is not to eliminate your anger; it is to change what you do with your anger. Counseling might be beneficial if you feel your anger has gotten out of control.

Pay attention to how your body reacts when you get angry. Does your face feel flushed? Do your hands shake? If you recognize your body's signals, you can intervene as your reaction begins. You will learn more about the impact of anger on your relationships and techniques for improving your relationships in chapter 10.

Achieve Spiritual Wellness

Only you can define your relationship with the world. Part of spiritual well-being is realizing that you and the people in the world are interconnected. You don't necessarily have to follow a particular religion to be spiritual. Spiritual well-being also means acknowledging that your choices affect other people. An important part of fostering spiritual well-being is taking the time to nurture your soul.

GET INVOLVED IN YOUR COMMUNITY

Going to an organized religious activity enhances your sense of community and oneness with others. You may have found from previous experiences that you could not sit still long enough to gain anything from a religious meeting. It is possible to find a spiritual group that fits your beliefs and has shorter services or allows movement during services.

You can also become connected to your community through volunteering with an altruistic organization. You can make a difference in the world by taking the focus off "me" and putting the focus on "we." Focusing on helping others can decrease feelings of depression.

Being creative is one of the positive aspects of having ADD. You can create wonderful ideas for an organization, and another member can help carry those ideas out. This matches the best of both worlds.

PRACTICE BEING GRATEFUL

During the day, you may encounter many irritations, including losing things, being disorganized, or having difficulty paying attention. It can be easy to forget what is going well in your life. Every night before bed, write in a journal five things you are thankful for. Also write down one thing that inspired you, one thing that surprised you, and one thing that touched you. By focusing on the positive, you put the irritations in perspective. You also ease the burdens of the day.

SPEND QUIET TIME ALONE

Find a place in your home where you can "escape." Even if you have a small living space, you can turn a corner into a sanctuary. Decorate it with calming artwork or objects. Make time to just be quiet and rest in this space. Try to keep others out of this space, especially when you are using it. Some of your best ideas and insights happen when you are quiet and reflective.

FIND YOUR PURPOSE

Part of practicing spiritual wellness is to discover the reason you are on the earth. Are you meant to discover something? Are you meant to be an advocate for a particular cause? Consider what legacy you want to leave. Ascribing meaning to your life allows you to put things in perspective. For resources to help you define your purpose, see the end of this chapter.

In this chapter, you learned the benefits of a balanced, healthy lifestyle. You also learned that finding your purpose in life is an important part of spiritual wellness. In the next chapter, you will learn how finding your purpose in life can also help you find a career that suits you.

Exercise: Discover Ways to Take Care of Yourself

When you are stressed, it can be easy to forget the ways that you are able to take care of yourself. For this exercise, write down healthy ways that you can reduce stress. Here are some ideas:

- taking a walk

- calling a friend

- playing sports

- taking a hot bath

- going to a movie

Find varied activities that can hold your interest. For more ideas, observe how others take care of themselves. Ask people with good stress management skills how they calm down. Look back to how you managed stress when you were a child. The next time you are feeling stress coming down on you, get out your list and practice one of the stress-relieving ideas you have written.

Resources

Adrienne, C. 2001. *Find Your Purpose, Change Your Life: Getting to the Heart of Your Life's Mission*. New York: Harper Paperbacks.

Davis, M., E. Eshelman, and M. McKay. 2008. *The Relaxation and Stress Reduction Workbook*. 6th ed. Oakland, CA: New Harbinger Publications.

EXERCISE APPS

Gym Technik
www.gymtechnik.com/blackberry/
(Blackberry)

iWorkout Lite
http://download.cnet.com/iWorkout-Lite/3000-2129
_4-10904932.html
(iPhone)

EXERCISE PARTNERS

Exercise Friends
www.exercisefriends.com

Find an Exercise Partner
www.findanexercisepartner.com

FOOD TRACKERS

LiveStrong.com MyPlate calorie counter
www.livestrong.com/thedailyplate/

MyFitnessPal calorie counter
www.myfitnesspal.com/

GENERAL FITNESS

American Council on Exercise
www.acefitness.org

American Dietetic Association
www.eatright.org

8

Find a Job That Fits You

In chapter 7, you learned about the physical, emotional, and spiritual dimensions of wellness. In this chapter, you will learn about another important dimension to having balance in your life: occupational wellness. Occupational wellness is being able to enjoy your work, having skills to search for jobs, and finding the job that is best suited to your skills and needs. It is also the ability to recognize opportunities for learning new skills.

People with ADD have a higher rate of changing jobs and being fired, and they tend to have lower incomes than people without ADHD, even when they have a similar education level (Barkley, Murphy, and Fischer 2008). People with ADD also miss more days of work due to "unofficial" absences (Secnik, Swensen, and Lage 2005). In many jobs, ADD works against you rather than serving as a strength. Not all jobs are created equal—at least not for people with ADD. People with ADD do best in jobs that

- are fast paced

- include different tasks each day

- allow you to move around during your workday

- include support from an assistant

- are intellectually stimulating

- take advantage of your ability to multitask

- have firm due dates for projects

- offer frequent feedback

- have clear expectations

- have a flexible schedule

- include interactions with various people

- offer immediate rewards for a job well done
  (for example, getting a big tip at a restaurant
  when you have provided good service)

In addition, it helps a lot if your boss has ADD or at least has an understanding of ADD.

Jobs such as firefighter, restaurant waitperson, teacher, emergency room physician, and trial attorney or positions in the military are good for people with ADD because they encompass many of the characteristics of ADD-friendly jobs. To determine whether your job is ADD friendly, consider how well it matches the characteristics listed above.

Examine Your Job Satisfaction

It is possible to love what you do for a living. When deciding if you want to continue in your current job, ask yourself the following questions:

- Do I look forward to my job in the morning?

- Is my ADD an asset or a liability in this job?

- Do I receive benefits at this job?

- Am I bored at this job?

- Does this job compromise my ethics and beliefs?

- Does this job help me work toward fulfilling my life's purpose?

For more guidance in determining your life's purpose, refer to chapter 7 or the resources at the end of this chapter.

Change Job Paths

Let's say you have decided you would like to seek a new job. People with ADD tend to jump into things, and then, when they realize what they have done, they pick up and move on. By defining your ideal job, you increase your chances of achieving success. Look on Internet job sites to get an idea of what jobs are available in your area of interest.

IDENTIFY YOUR IDEAL JOB

Finding a new job takes some introspection. To clarify your interests and skills, ask yourself the following questions:

- What did I want to be when I was a kid?

- What did I enjoy doing in school?

- What are my best skills and abilities?

- What do I like to do for fun?

- What do my family and friends say are my best qualities?

Discover Your Job Values

What do you value most in a job? To some people, it is very important that they earn a high income. Others value a job that involves physical activity. Do you value a feeling of job security, variety in your workday, or the opportunity to help others? Explore the top three values that are most important to you. See if the job you are interested in matches these three values. If not, it may not be the best job for you.

Shadow Someone

When you find a job that sparks your interest, you may go full steam ahead, then quit after a month because it was totally different than you expected. One way to avoid this is to shadow someone with the same job before accepting the position. "Shadowing" means attending at least part of a person's workday so you get a realistic sense of what the job entails. You can find someone in your field by asking for a referral, searching your online college alumni website, or through a university career counseling center.

When talking to someone whose job interests you, ask the following questions:

- What is your typical day like?

- What level of education do you need for this job?

- What skills do you need for this job?

- What personality characteristics do you need for this job?

- How important is the ability to be organized in this job?

- What is the best thing about your job?

- What would you change about your job?

- How did you find this job?

Find a Job That Fits Your Sleep Cycle

Your previous jobs may not have worked for you because you were meant to be alert at night and sleep during the day. As you read in chapters 5 and 7, people with ADD can tend to be night owls. If you are more alert at night, find a job where being a night owl is a prerequisite. Good jobs for night owls include night-shift nursing, firefighting, and providing computer technical support.

Consider Working at Home

Every year, more people are choosing to work from their home. It can be exciting for people with ADD to start their own business or work for a company from the comfort of their own home. They can set flexible hours, avoid commuting to work, and have more autonomy. However, people who work from home need to be self-motivated and manage time well, areas where people with ADD have difficulty. Consider whether you have the drive and structure in your life to be successful working from home before you take the plunge.

SEEK OUTSIDE HELP WITH YOUR JOB SEARCH

Just as an organization buddy can help you overcome clutter, an outside party can provide valuable support and guidance in your job search. One way to determine which job is best for you is to get career counseling. You can find career counselors in private practice, working at an agency, or affiliated with a college or university. You may also be able to find career counseling online.

DISCOVER YOUR PERSONALITY TYPE

Your personality type is a set of related characteristics that describe you. You can discover your personality type by completing assessments with job counselors or on your own. Not only can you discover which jobs are best for your personality type, you can also discover how your personality type influences relationships, family life, and learning style. For more information on job assessment and personality type, see the resources at the end of this chapter.

CONSIDER GOING BACK TO SCHOOL

Many people with ADD are chronically underemployed. This means that you have more intelligence and ability than your job requires. This leads to a great deal of boredom. People with ADD may be underemployed because they could not focus in school in order to get a diploma or degree. Going back to school may lead to a job you love.

This time around, school can be a positive experience. First of all, you now have more awareness about your ADD.

You may also now be taking medication for ADD, which can greatly improve your school performance. You have the option of obtaining accommodations at your school. Colleges and universities have support centers for students with disabilities.

Furthering your education may cost money and require you to live pretty lean for a few years, but it is an investment—in yourself. In the long term, you will have a higher-paying job and gain even more skills. Check with your local community college about going back to school. If you did not receive your high school diploma, you can earn a general equivalency diploma (GED) and then continue on to higher education.

Look outside the usual college experience. Online college programs and weekend classes are available for people who need to work full-time while getting their degree. Expand on your skills by obtaining further training in your field. Also look into courses on computer skills. These skills are sought after by employers.

Make the Most of Your Job Search

If your current job is not ADD-friendly or does not match your life's purpose, it's time to start on a job search. Difficulties with organization can make job hunting overwhelming and chaotic. In this section, the tasks of a job search have been broken down into smaller, more manageable pieces. Approaching your job search using simple steps makes the process more manageable and productive.

LET PEOPLE KNOW YOU ARE LOOKING

Being referred by people you know is the best way to get a job. Tell everyone you know that you are looking for a job. Tell them what you are interested in and what skills you possess. You never know when a friend of a friend might have a job opening.

MAINTAIN A CURRENT RÉSUMÉ

Your résumé is a valuable piece of information for prospective employers. It tells employers your work history, education level, and skills. Keep your résumé up to date by typing in events immediately after they happen. If you wait to update your résumé, you will inevitably forget some important items.

Spelling and grammar errors on résumés are the kiss of death. Any résumé with errors is likely to go in the prospective employer's circular file (trash basket). Using spell-check on your résumé is not enough. Spell-check does not catch everything. Have your partner, roommate, or a job counselor review your résumé. You can post your résumé on job-hunting websites so that employers from around the world will be able to view your résumé.

USE ONLINE RESOURCES

If you are unemployed, get the word out on your social networking sites that you're looking for a job. (Note: if you are currently employed, this may not be a good idea. Your current employer may hear through the grapevine or discover on the Internet that you may be leaving soon.) Also look at your college's alumni website. Many alumni websites have online forums for people looking for work or looking to hire. You can also look for jobs and post your résumé on online job boards. More information on online job search resources can be found at the end of this chapter.

CARRY BUSINESS CARDS WITH YOU

Business cards help people remember you and more easily get in contact with you. They need not be expensive. You can make them on your computer using special printer paper, or you can use a printing company. Some online printing companies not only have reasonable prices but also have templates for business cards and will let you upload your own images. Include your address, phone numbers, e-mail, website, and professional networking address. Write your areas of interest on your card. Always carry cards. You never know when you will run into someone who has a job lead for you.

BRUSH UP ON YOUR INTERVIEW SKILLS

The purpose of a job interview is for the prospective employer to get to know you and determine if you're a good fit for the position. Equally important, it's an opportunity for you to evaluate whether the job is a good match for your skills, personality, and values. Here's how to show your best side during an interview.

Do Your Homework

Do some research on the company before your interview. You can review information about larger companies on investment websites and on the companies' own websites. Also read business newspapers, such as *The Wall Street Journal*. See the resources at the end of this chapter for more information.

Come up with a salary amount you feel you are worth. This is almost always asked of you at a job interview. Research the salaries for that type of position before the interview. Take into account your years of experience when coming up with a salary figure.

Be Prepared

Practice your interview skills. Have a friend play the part of the interviewer. Have your friend critique your performance. Here are some common interview questions:

- Why do you want to leave your current job?

- How would you describe yourself?

- What are your strengths and weaknesses?

- How do you deal with stress?

- Why should we hire you?

Be Professional

When selecting clothes for an interview, dress like you already have the job. If you are interviewing for an office position, dress professionally. For both men and women, wearing a two-piece suit in a neutral color (navy or gray) is best. Take some deep breaths right before the interview and try just to be yourself. Being genuine comes across much better to prospective employers. Be confident that you have the abilities and personality that this job requires. After the interview, write a thank-you note to the interviewers (a real thank-you note, not an e-mail). Thank them for the opportunity to meet with them, and include that you have a great deal of interest in their company.

Work with Your ADD, Not Against It

Once you have found a job that fits your skills, interests, and educational level, you need to consider whether you need accommodations to be effective and happy in your work.

Accommodations are ways that you can adjust your environment to make it easier to focus and be efficient at your job. You can get accommodations by

- making adjustments to your work space and work habits on your own,

- asking your employer for accommodations, or

- seeking accommodations through the legal system if neither of those options is possible.

The more accommodations you can arrange on your own, the less you will need to disclose your ADD to your employer or face legal struggles with your employer.

LEARN THE UNWRITTEN RULES OF THE OFFICE

Many workplaces have employee manuals, but there are also subtle, unspoken rules about how things operate. For example, a secretary may have more influence than her boss in getting things done. People with ADD can have a lot of difficulty learning the unwritten rules. To learn these rules, observe how other people in the office behave. When you are more comfortable in your work environment, ask someone in the know about how certain processes are conducted.

TRY THESE ACCOMMODATIONS FOR THE WORKPLACE

Here are some simple ways to make your job and workplace more ADD friendly:

- Take breaks during your workday, even if it is just to walk outside for a few minutes.

- Take a walk during your lunch break.

- When scheduling your workday, allow extra time for meetings and other work events so you do not overbook yourself.

- If at all possible, hire an administrative assistant to help with organization and detailed paperwork.

- Ask for an office that is relatively free from distractions. An office that is out of the main working area is ideal.

- Turn off e-mail/text/social networking notifications (sounds and flashing lights) on your phone.

- Avoid working in a cubicle. There are too many distractions.

- If distractions are unavoidable, wear earplugs or noise-canceling headphones while you work.

- Use a white noise machine to block out auditory distractions.

- During meetings, keep your hands busy. Concentrating your physical energy will make it easier for you to focus. This technique is called *concentrated distraction*.

- If your employer does not assign deadlines, create your own.

- Break large projects into smaller tasks.

- Arrive early or stay late to do paperwork, when there are fewer distractions.

- When coworkers tell you they need something from you, ask them to e-mail it to you so you not only are reminded of it but also have a written record of the request.

- Get requests and orders in writing when possible. Keeping a paper (or e-mail) trail helps protect you and your job.

- When your employer gives you an assignment, repeat the request in your own words to make sure you understood correctly.

- Difficulty with remembering names is common in people with ADD. To remember the names of the people in your office, draw a diagram of the office layout, including individual offices. Write in your coworkers' names in the locations where they work. You can also have a picture of the person attached to their contact information in your phone or e-mail contact software.

- Ask your employer for feedback about your performance. Get this feedback in writing. The next time you meet with your employer for a review, bring the feedback sheet from the last review.

- Post a dry-erase board on your office wall. When you think of an important idea, immediately write it down. Write it in red if it is urgent.

- Leave yourself voicemail messages or e-mails if you need to remember something for the next day.

- If you are a teacher, have your students make name tags for their desks. You no longer need to spend brainpower remembering your students' names.

Disclosing Your ADD

When deciding whether to disclose your ADD, consider whether the benefits of telling your employer outweigh the risks. First try to make your own accommodations. If you need additional accommodations, work directly with your employer. Seeking legal recourse is a last resort. Keep in mind that legal action is a long and expensive process.

If you have ADD, you may be protected by the Americans with Disabilities Act and the Rehabilitation Act of 1973. These laws prohibit discrimination due to a disability such as ADD. However, you are not automatically covered by these laws. To be covered, you must disclose to your employer that you have ADD. Try to work with your employer directly before considering legal action.

In this chapter, you learned what types of jobs are more amenable to people with ADD. You also learned how to discern the unwritten rules of the workplace and how to ask for what you need from your employers. In chapter 9, you will learn more about using good social skills to help you on the road to success.

Exercise: Explore Your Job History

One of the best ways to help yourself find an ideal job is by looking back over the jobs that did not work out for you. For each job you have had, write down the following:

- your title

- name of the company

- dates you worked at the job

- reason for leaving

- whether you liked the job, and why or why not

It can be difficult to remember specific details of all your jobs, but the most important thing is to identify why you left each job. Look at the list for a pattern in your reasons for leaving.

- Did you leave jobs mainly because you were bored, or did you get fired?

- Did you leave the jobs on good terms, or did you walk out?

Once you know which jobs you liked and which you didn't like—and why—you can make a more insightful decision when choosing your future job.

Resources

Bolles, R. 2010. *What Color Is Your Parachute? 2011: A Practical Manual for Job-Hunters and Career-Changers*. Berkeley: Ten Speed Press.

Post, P. 2005. *Emily Post's The Etiquette Advantage in Business: Personal Skills for Professional Success*. 2nd ed. New York: William Morrow.

Tieger, P., and B. Barron-Tieger. 2007. *Do What You Are: Discover the Perfect Career for You Through the Secrets of Personality Type*. 4th ed. Boston: Little, Brown.

Americans with Disabilities Act (ADA)
U.S. Department of Justice
www.ada.gov/

Linked In
www.linkedin.com

National Career Development Association
www.ncda.org

The Wall Street Journal
www.wsj.com
(800) 975-8609

U.S. Department of Labor, Bureau of Labor Statistics
Occupational Outlook Handbook. www.bls.gov/oco

Vistaprint
www.vistaprint.com

Improve Your Social Skills

I n chapter 8, you learned about the importance of occupational wellness. You also learned about accommodations you can make so that your job is more ADD-friendly. In this chapter, you will learn about social wellness. Social wellness includes the ability to interact with a variety of people, communicate effectively, and develop friendships.

Quell Your Feelings of Rejection

People with ADD often take rejection very personally. This may stem from childhood, when you may have felt ostracized by other children. You may have been teased or picked last for teams, or perhaps you did not get invited to birthday parties. The hardest part is that you probably did not know why you were being treated this way.

Do you feel as if you were not in line the day the social skills manuals were handed out? Did it seem like everyone else knew unwritten rules or a special code that they did not share with you? As a child with ADD, you probably did not pick up on social skills like other children. You may not have been able to pay attention well enough to notice the social behaviors of other children. Or you may have been punished at school by being kept inside at recess, which limited your opportunities to learn social skills. You may not have been taking medication for ADD. Medication greatly improves the ability to learn social skills.

Social skills are like building blocks. When you aren't able to get the first row of blocks set up early in life, it is very difficult—if not impossible—to build on top of them. This lack of social knowledge can lead you to feel embarrassed, shy, depressed, or anxious. By learning the skills in this chapter, you can start stacking up the building blocks again—this time with success.

Use Active Listening Skills

Active listening skills are techniques that let people know that you are paying attention and understanding what they are saying, leading to more enriching relationships.

LISTEN WITH YOUR BODY

Sit directly facing the other person. Keep your arms and legs uncrossed. When you cross your arms when you are listening to someone, it appears as if you are bored or upset by what the person has said. Make eye contact. This means looking at the person but not staring intently. It is okay to break eye contact for very brief moments.

Use body language to convey to the person how you are feeling about the topic. If you are in agreement, nod your head.

If you cannot believe what has happened to the person, shake your head. Saying "I see" or "go on" lets the person know you are following what's being said.

REPEAT BACK WHAT SOMEONE HAS SAID

Part of a good relationship is that both people feel they are being heard. *Paraphrasing* is when you repeat back what someone has told you, only you use your own words. For example, your friend tells you, "I feel horrible. I was stood up last night by my date." You might say, "Oh, no! She didn't show up?" Paraphrasing helps both you and your conversation partner. You are more likely to pay attention and remember what your friend has said, and your friend will feel like you are listening.

This technique also works when you are given instructions. It is very hard for people with ADD to remember multi-step directions. When people give you instructions, try saying, "Let me make sure I've got this right," and repeat the instructions back to them. This method of making sure you understood someone is called *echoing*. The person will correct you if you misunderstood or forgot one of the instructions. If it is difficult for you to remember to repeat instructions, tell your boss or your friends that you would appreciate it if they would ask you to repeat the instructions back to them.

Learn How to Read Nonverbal Communication

There are two types of communication: verbal and nonverbal. *Verbal communication* is the words and vocalizations you use to communicate. Both sighing and saying, "I am so frustrated" are examples of verbal communication. *Nonverbal communication* is how you get your point across without opening your mouth. For example, a way to express *I am so frustrated* without words is to put your head in your hands. People do not just talk with words; they also talk with their facial expressions and body language. For example, if someone says, "I really value your opinion" while he rolls his eyes, chances are he may not be that interested in your opinion.

Recognizing nonverbal communication is one of the executive functions of the brain, which you learned about in chapter 1. People with ADD have problems interpreting the meaning of nonverbal communication, including figuring out people's emotions just from their facial expressions (Uekermann et al. 2010). For example, you may be talking too much and not notice that the person you are talking to is checking her watch or yawning. Because you do not notice this, you continue talking. You may also not notice when someone is getting visibly upset with you, or the opposite could happen—you could interpret a neutral facial expression as one of boredom or upset.

When someone is speaking to you, try to notice not only their verbal message but also their nonverbal message. This can take some practice, but once you understand the meaning of a nonverbal message, it will be easier to interpret next time.

Make a Good First Impression

While you may think it is superficial to judge someone by how they look, it is also a fact of life. People with ADD may wear wrinkled clothes because they forgot to iron them or just did not have time. Look into buying wrinkle-free clothes. They are a good investment because they will help you make a better first impression. This can lead to more social and professional success.

When you have ADD and you're engrossed in conversation, it can be difficult to know when you are being socially inappropriate. There are different ways to monitor your social behavior. Some compensation techniques involve preparing before social contact, while others can be used in the midst of conversation.

People with ADD can have difficulty determining how close to someone they should stand when they are talking. You may stand too close for the other person's comfort, and he may step away from you. Then you step closer, and he steps back. Pretty soon he is backed up to a wall.

USE THE HULA HOOP TEST

While appropriate social distance is largely determined by a person's culture, the general guideline is approximately the width of a hula hoop. You can practice this distance with a partner and a hula hoop. Get a good idea of the distance between you and the other person when there is a hula hoop between you. The next time you are engaged in conversation, notice whether there is enough space between the two of you.

LET PEOPLE KNOW WHEN YOU ARE SWITCHING TRACKS

You may bring up unrelated topics in conversation. Perhaps the conversation was starting to bore you, or you felt you had to bring up this new topic quickly so you did not forget it. The other person may have difficulty following a topic that seems to come out of the blue. When you are going to change topics or switch tracks, give a verbal heads-up. Simply say, "I'm changing topics" or "I'm switching tracks on you." This gives the other person a moment to adjust. They will appreciate your consideration.

USE A NONVERBAL SIGNAL

When you are talking with a small group, you may tend to ramble, talk too loudly, or interrupt others. An unobtrusive way to learn when you do these things is to devise subtle nonverbal signals with a friend. Your friend can then use these signals (for example, scratching her neck, tugging her earlobe, or coughing) when you show one of the offending behaviors. The nice part is that only you and your friend will be aware of the signals. Set up a different signal for each "social infraction," so you know exactly what you need to fix.

BE AWARE OF YOUR VOICE MODULATION

Has anyone ever told you that you were talking too loud or too fast? When you have ADD, it can be difficult to pace yourself. It may feel as if the words and the volume of speech are a runaway train. Be aware of the signals people give when you are talking too loud. They may step back or excuse themselves from the conversation. If people ask you to slow down, that's an obvious cue that you are talking too fast. They may also look like they are concentrating a little too intently on what you are saying. You can ask friends to let you know if you are talking too fast.

ACKNOWLEDGE WHEN YOU INTERRUPT

A feature of ADD is the need to state an idea as soon as it comes into your head, before you forget it. Sometimes this need causes people with ADD to interrupt others. If you catch yourself interrupting, stop what you are saying and apologize. You can also tell your conversation partner that you have an idea that you need to tell them or else it will leave your mind. Medication for ADD can be especially helpful for people who interrupt. Medications help you retain ideas until it is your turn to talk. They also decrease impulsivity, making it easier to stop yourself from interrupting.

LEARN THE ART OF SMALL TALK

Engaging in small talk not only helps you meet new people, it also helps expand your network of contacts. Small talk is the art of starting conversations with people by asking about innocuous topics. You may think, *I don't have the time or patience for small talk. What's the point?* The point is this: You wouldn't start your car in fifth gear, would you? You will make much more progress by getting to know someone gradually instead of jumping right in with what you need from them. A person might find it uncouth if you started a conversation with "Is your company hiring?" Small talk helps people ease into a social relationship. It's part of the social dance in which we all participate.

You can start small talk by complimenting people on what they are wearing or making a comment about the activity in which you both are participating. You could say, "I like your sweater" or "There was a really good turnout tonight." The person will answer you and may make additional conversation with you. That's how small talk evolves into a social conversation.

You may make small talk with someone who either ignores you or gives you a very short answer and then walks away. Do not take this personally. Some people will not respond positively to small talk. They may be shy, or they may not be able to hear you. Just try again with a new person. If you have a friend with you, ask how you did with your small talk. Your friend can give valuable feedback and may be able to explain why a person responded a certain way.

KNOW WHEN A CONVERSATION IS ENDING

It may be difficult for you to pick up on signals that people use when they are done talking with you. They may tell you that they need to get some food or a drink. This is not an invitation to go with them unless they expressly ask you. They may tell you that it was nice talking with you or that they will talk to you later. You can also tell that it is time to end the conversation when you notice people are looking around or are losing eye contact with you. If you notice these nonverbal behaviors, politely say, "It was nice meeting you" and excuse yourself.

SAVE YOURSELF FROM FORGETTING NAMES

It can be very difficult for people with ADD to remember people's names. Sometimes you can be so focused on making a good impression and showing good social skills that the name of the person you just met slips out of your mind.

Let's say a friend joins the conversation and wants to meet the person to whom you are talking. How do you introduce someone when you do not remember his name? There are a few solutions to this problem. First, you can simply introduce the person whose name you cannot remember to your friend ("Let me introduce you to Jane"). You could also just be honest. Say, "I'm sorry. I have difficulty remembering names. Would you mind telling me your name again?" People will usually appreciate your honesty, and it is better than calling someone by the wrong name. Another technique is to tell the two people, "I'll let you introduce yourselves." Finally, you can go off to the side and quietly ask someone else the person's name.

When you first meet people, repeat their name back to them. This solidifies the person's name in your mind. For example, a colleague says, "Hello, I'm Jim. Nice to meet you." You would respond, "Hello, Jim. It's nice to meet you, too." It may feel awkward at first to use a new method of talking with people, but with time it will get easier.

Not only can people with ADD have difficulty remembering names, they also can have difficulty recognizing people. This is called *facial blindness*. If you find yourself unable to recognize someone, be honest and say that you have difficulty matching names with faces. Being honest with another person can help ease your tension. You can also attach a picture of the person with their contact information in your phone or your e-mail contacts. When the person calls you, her name and face pops up. It's a great way to connect the name with the face.

Learn to Be Assertive

Like many people with ADD who have suffered past rejections and desperately want to make friends, you may have difficulty standing up for your rights. You may be afraid that if you upset people, they will no longer like you. However, you are not being good to yourself or to others if you let them treat you poorly.

Many times people with ADD have a feeling that the other person is okay and they are not okay. This is called being *passive*. You respect the other person's needs more than your needs. You allow people to take advantage of you, and you do not speak up for your rights. The opposite of being passive is being *aggressive*. This is a feeling that the other person is not okay but you are okay. You respect your needs and not the other person's needs. A person who is aggressive may not show respect to other people, may call them names, or may even get into physical fights. The goal is to be right in the middle between being passive and being aggressive. This middle ground is being *assertive*. This means that you feel like the other person is okay and you are okay. You respect both yourself and the other person equally.

USE "I FEEL" STATEMENTS

Using "I feel" statements is a good assertiveness technique. Let's say your friend has invited you to the movies. Your friend says, "Let's go see *The Blood and Gore Film Fest* at MegaCinema 26." You really do not like horror movies. A passive answer would be, "Sure, I'll go." But you would be grossed out and unhappy watching the movie. An aggressive statement would be, "I can't believe you'd watch those disgusting movies. What kind of creep are you?" You are letting your friend know you do not want to go see that movie, but you are also criticizing your friend and questioning his judgment. An assertive response would be, "I really feel uncomfortable watching horror movies. How about if we go see a comedy instead?" This way, you are letting your friend know that you are not interested in horror movies but you still want to spend time with him. You are also offering an alternative that you both might enjoy.

For resources on assertiveness skills, see the end of the chapter.

Learn Proper Etiquette

If you feel socially awkward, learning proper etiquette can make things a little easier. When you know proper etiquette, you know how to hold your knife and fork correctly, and you know how to politely respond to people. You can learn proper etiquette through books and even classes in your community. See the end of this chapter for resources for learning etiquette.

In this chapter, you will learn two of the most important parts of proper social etiquette: being gracious and speaking the truth diplomatically.

BE GRACIOUS

Good social skills include a sense of gratitude toward others. When someone gives you a gift, write a thank-you note the same day. On occasions like birthday parties or gift showers, have someone write down a description of each gift and the name of the person who gave you the gift.

Always have thank-you cards available so you can write the notes as soon as possible. Note that it is good manners to actually write this note by hand rather than e-mailing it. When writing a thank-you note, first describe the gift. This shows the gift-giver that you put special thought into your thank-you note, and it shows your appreciation for the gift. Next, write about either where you will be displaying the gift or how you will be using the gift. Finally, thank the gift-giver again. Here is an example:

Dear Aunt Sadie,

Thank you very much for the lovely swan made out of toothpicks. I have put it on display in my china cabinet for everyone to see. Thank you again for such a thoughtful gift.

Love,

Stephanie

Even if you do not like a gift, thank the giver anyway. It is the gesture of a gift, not the actual gift, that is most important. A little thank-you goes a long way.

When you are invited to someone's home for dinner or a party, bring a gift for the host or hostess. Ideas for gifts include a bottle of wine, flowers, or a picture frame. You can also ask the host or hostess ahead of time what food they might need for the event. Also write a thank-you note after you return from the event.

SPEAK THE TRUTH DIPLOMATICALLY

People with ADD can be some of the most honest people—sometimes to the point that they say things that are too harsh. Being diplomatic means being able to get your point across without upsetting someone. It means that you can be honest without being harsh. If a friend asks you if you like her dress, it would be rude to respond with, "You know, you look really bad in red." However, you can say, "I think I like the blue dress better." This is more helpful and gets your point across as well. You are still being honest; you are just phrasing it in a nicer way.

LEARN APPROPRIATE TECHNOLOGY ETIQUETTE

Monitor what you post on social networking sites. Never disclose that you are not home or on vacation. Remember to be respectful of others. The saying "If you can't say something nice, don't say anything at all" is important to remember when posting comments on people's profiles or posts. And remember, once something is posted online, it is there forever—even after you delete it.

Put your phone on silent or vibrate when you are in public settings such as at a movie or in a restaurant. Also put your phone away when you are socializing with other people. Subjecting everyone to your extracurricular social outreach (talking on the phone, checking Facebook, or texting while someone is trying to talk to you) is a surefire way of annoying others.

Exercise: Role-Play Social Situations

Get together with a friend who has good social skills. By using a technique called role-playing, you can act out a social situation before the actual event occurs. You play yourself, and your friend plays another character. Role-play the following vignettes:

- You are introducing yourself to some new business associates.

- At a bar, you see an attractive person you'd like to meet.

- You accidentally trip someone as they are walking past you.

- You go to the dry cleaner to pick up your clothes, and you are not given the discount they promised you last time.

- You need to talk to someone who is busy in a conversation with another person.

Afterward, have your friend critique your "performance." What did you do well? What needs work? Then switch roles. Have your friend be you, while you play the other character. Notice how your friend handles these social situations. Discuss afterward the techniques she used. Talk with your friend about why she said certain things or behaved in certain ways. You can learn a great deal by doing this "as if" exercise.

In this chapter, you learned how to sharpen your social skills, an area in which people with ADD can have great difficulty. Remember to reward yourself for any progress you are making. If you ever feel unsure how to proceed socially, look at what everyone else is doing. Observation can be the best teacher. Challenge yourself to participate actively in social situations. Even if you make an error, you will be okay, and you will learn from the experience.

Good social skills lead to important relationships. In chapter 10, you will learn how to enrich these relationships through effective communication and intimacy-building skills. You will also learn the importance of social reciprocity.

Resources

Alberti, R. E., and M. L. Emmons. 2008. *Your Perfect Right: Assertiveness and Equality in Your Life and Relationships.* 9th ed. Atascadero, CA: Impact Publishers.

Novotni, M. 1999. *What Does Everyone Know That I Don't? Social Skills Help for Adults with Attention Deficit/Hyperactivity Disorder (AD/HD).* Plantation, FL: Specialty Press.

Post, P. 2004. *Emily Post's Etiquette.* 17th ed. New York: HarperResource.

10

Enrich Your Relationships

In chapter 9, you learned techniques for improving your social skills. Social skills are the building blocks for all relationships. While social skills can help you begin relationships, maintaining relationships can be difficult when you have ADD.

People with ADD are more likely to get divorced and have multiple marriages (Weiss, Hechtman, and Weiss 1999). This may be because people who don't have ADD frequently misinterpret the behavior of a partner with ADD. For example, a woman whose husband has ADD might believe that he does not care about her because he forgot her birthday. This trend in divorce and remarriage may also be due to the fact that people with ADD get bored easily and like variety. This can lead to extramarital affairs, which lead to divorce. Or people with ADD may get divorced simply because they are bored and want to move on.

In this chapter, you will learn about each of these relationship issues that face people with ADD. You will learn preventive techniques to help you form healthy, lasting relationships.

Be Aware That Your Actions May Be Misinterpreted

Forgetfulness, interrupting, and abruptness may be interpreted by others as being rude and uncaring. However, these behaviors are related to having ADD. While ADD is not an excuse for these behaviors, it does give insight into why you act the way you do.

Because the majority of people do not have ADD, these behaviors are not considered socially acceptable. Others' misinterpretation of your behaviors can affect your relationships. Suppose that you forgot to pick up some milk at the store. Your spouse may take it personally, believing you did not care about what she was asking you to do. However, you know that you just forgot to get the milk because you were trying to remember a whole bunch of different items at the same time.

When your spouse requests something from you, use the technique you learned earlier: repeat back what your spouse has requested. This not only helps you clarify what your spouse needs from you, it also cements the information in your brain. It also conveys that you are listening and care about your spouse's needs.

EDUCATE OTHERS ABOUT ADD

People become frustrated and upset by things they do not understand. There is a good chance that the important people in your life do not know the symptoms and resulting behaviors that are a part of ADD. By educating people about ADD, you open a new door to improved communication and understanding.

Give your loved ones this book. Tell them it will help them understand what things are like in the "ADD world."

Acknowledge to your loved ones that you understand that they get frustrated when you do certain things. Let them know that these events are equally frustrating to you and that you are not trying to upset them. Also refer them to the books and websites that are listed at the end of chapter 1.

TALK ABOUT YOUR DIAGNOSIS

Whether or not you disclose your ADD diagnosis to someone depends largely on the amount of trust you have in the person. You want to be fairly certain that your family and friends will keep your diagnosis in confidence and that they will listen in a nonjudgmental way. When you disclose that you have ADD to a family member or friend, let her know that you would like the information to be kept just between the two of you. Be aware, however, that confidentiality cannot be guaranteed. Unfortunately, there is still stigma surrounding mental health issues; but for the most part, you should find plenty of support.

If you feel uncomfortable telling your family and friends about the diagnosis of ADD, consider just mentioning some areas in which you could use support. For instance, you could ask for help in staying organized and cutting back on the number of interruptions during a conversation. Be specific about how this person can support you—by just listening to you, taking a walk with you during breaks from tasks, or even just giving you a hug when you need one.

You may wonder if you should tell your child about your ADD diagnosis. For older children and teenagers, it may be very helpful to share that information, including educating them about the genetic basis of ADD. It's especially important to explain to your child that having untreated ADD may lead to substance abuse, depression, anxiety, and eating disorders more so than for people without ADD. It is important to emphasize to your child that he should feel free to talk to you any time if something is concerning him. Just knowing a parent is available to talk can make a huge difference in a child's life.

You also want to let your children know how important it is to take safety precautions (such as wearing a helmet or fastening a seat belt) before engaging in activities. This is a priority because people (especially children) with ADD are more prone to injury and accidents than people without ADD (Sabuncuoglu 2007; Thompson, Molina, Pelham, and Gnagy 2007).

Be aware that anything you tell your child may be shared with others. Be especially cautious discussing your use of medication to your children, particularly if you take stimulant medication. You want to make sure that your medication stays safe and secure. Even if your child may not try to get access to your medication, his friends might.

ASK THE MAGIC QUESTION

The next time someone is upset with you and you do not know what you did to cause the person to be angry, ask, "What do you need from me right now?" This gives the person a second to think about a solution, and it helps diffuse the anger. The person's answer will help clarify what happened. You may discover that the person was not even upset with you after all. It can also be helpful for loved ones to ask you this question when they are unsure about your needs.

NOTICE WHEN YOU ARE PERSONALIZING

People with ADD can be very sensitive to rejection. They can also be sensitive to people's moods. You may think that someone is angry with you when in fact her mood has nothing to do with you. When you are feeling that because someone gave you a "mean" look, you must have done something to him, you are *personalizing*. You are attributing meaning to someone's behavior. It is easy to fall into the personalizing trap when you have had difficulties with people criticizing you or rejecting you. Remind yourself that you don't always have to take things personally. Even if someone is mad at you, it may be the other person's problem, not yours.

RESPOND EFFECTIVELY TO THE "CRUTCH" QUESTION

Sometimes you will encounter friends and family who think that you really do not have ADD and you are using the label of ADD as an excuse or "crutch" for your behaviors. If you explain that you interrupt because you have ADD, they may respond, "Do you take responsibility for anything, or do you just blame it on ADD?" An assertive reply is "I am taking responsibility by telling you that I have ADD. While that does not excuse my behavior, it does give you insight as to why I do some of the things I do."

You may also have people tell you that you do not have ADD, that you're just lazy and unmotivated. It can be especially painful when loved ones criticize you this way since you know how hard you have tried to compensate for your ADD. You could respond by saying, "Telling me I am lazy does not help me. I feel hurt when someone says that I am lazy, because I am working hard to make my life better." Phrasing your response in an "I feel" statement is an effective way of telling someone how you feel without being judgmental.

Sometimes people become frustrated and upset about things they don't understand. If your family or friends feel you were misdiagnosed, talk to them about it. Provide facts about ADD, such as its genetic and biological origins, pointing out that several genes for ADD have been identified. You will get much further in educating others if you keep a calm and steady demeanor and present the facts about ADD.

Learn Social Reciprocity

Social reciprocity is just a fancy way of saying "If you do something for me, I'll do something for you." Often, people with ADD either give too much or take too much in relationships. This can leave a relationship feeling lopsided. To understand social reciprocity, consider the concept of chips in the bank.

PUT CHIPS IN THE BANK

When you go to the bank and deposit money, you expect that you will be able to withdraw that money when you need it. But what if you went to the bank and they told you there was no money in your account? You wouldn't be able to make any withdrawals. This is very much like relationships.

When you ask a friend for a favor, you are withdrawing chips from her bank. If you have not deposited any chips in your friend's bank by helping her out or being nice to her, she is less likely to let you withdraw chips from her bank (do favors for you). Keep an eye on your "chip totals" in other people's banks. A healthy relationship balances give and take.

AVOID PEOPLE TAKING ADVANTAGE OF YOU

The opposite can happen, too: you can give away too many chips. When you have ADD and you've had difficulty making friends, you may want other people to like you. A friend may ask you over and over to help him out, but when you need a favor from him, he turns you down. Instead of helping him out and then getting angry at how he never does the same for you, ask yourself if this relationship is a healthy one.

Learn How to Compromise

There is a saying, "You can either be married or be right." Compromise means that everyone wins. However, you both have to be willing to make changes in order to compromise. There are two areas where you may need to compromise in your relationship: activities that you both can enjoy and household chores.

FIND ACTIVITIES THAT EVERYONE CAN ENJOY

For most people, an ideal vacation would be spent relaxing and "doing nothing." However, a vacation like this could really irritate a person with ADD. You may prefer to be busy doing something almost all the time. You may pack extra things to do just so you don't get bored.

However, you and your loved ones can make a compromise. You can find a vacation that incorporates learning and active pursuits while also encouraging relaxation. "Learning vacations" incorporate activities such as cooking classes, cultural tours, spas, archaeology, and nature study. These vacations offer the best of both worlds: they provide intellectual stimulation and activities for people with ADD and can also be relaxing for other members of the family.

DELEGATE HOUSEHOLD CHORES

In chapter 5, you learned that delegating tasks is important for good time management. While dividing up chores is a good idea, it may not be easy for you to remember to do the chores. Your spouse might get irritated with reminding you to do a chore. To remind yourself, put a chore schedule on your refrigerator. Sit down with your spouse and decide which chores each of you would prefer to do. Maybe you would enjoy mowing the lawn more than doing the laundry.

If the number of chores seems insurmountable, maybe you and your spouse can let some things go. Is it really that important that the kitchen counters are wiped off every day? If you can afford it, have a cleaning service come in once a week. It is worth the peace it brings to your home.

Control Your Anger

In chapter 7, you learned how people with ADD can have difficulties with anger. Anger reactions can happen more quickly in people with ADD. Things that don't really bother other people can get you very upset. People tend to let out their anger on the people closest to them: their family. For people with ADD, anger can be like a runaway train barreling down the tracks. They don't know how much damage they have caused until it's too late.

TAKE A TIME-OUT

Dumping your anger on loved ones may initially be a relief, and it may feel good temporarily. However, after you have cooled down, you will feel guilt and remorse. Your family can become traumatized by your temper.

Here's a way to prevent a meltdown. If you feel you are about to lose your cool, give yourself a time-out. Have a room in the house where you can go when you get angry. Let your family know ahead of time that if you are in this room with the door shut, they are not to disturb you, and you are allowed to stay in there as long as you need to. When you feel you are ready to talk to the person who upset you, use "I feel" statements.

You may go with family or friends to a place where you feel overwhelmed. This can happen in a store where there is a lot of sensory stimulation: bright lights, intercom announcements, and crowds. If you feel you are reaching a point of sensory overload, tell the people you are with that you need a break because you are feeling overwhelmed. Tell them that you will be waiting outside or in the car. Tell them whether you need to go home or you are okay with them spending some more time in the store. It is better to excuse yourself than to stay in the store and become increasingly irritable.

SCHEDULE FIGHTS

The best relationships are not ones without arguments; in fact, couples who argue effectively have a better chance for a successful relationship. Arguing effectively is the key. Do you ever find yourself arguing with your partner over and over about the same issues and never coming to a conclusion? The goal of effective arguing is to get your point of view heard and hopefully reach a compromise.

Schedule an "argument time" once a week. Select your topic ahead of time. Then set a timer for fifteen minutes. Using the "I feel" statements you learned in chapter 9, say how you feel about the issue. When the timer goes off, it's your partner's turn—even if you haven't finished talking. Reset the timer for fifteen minutes. Your partner then uses "I feel" statements to describe how he feels about the issue. When the timer goes off, you are done discussing the topic. Even if you don't reach a solution within those thirty minutes, you are airing your feelings and opening communication. A solution will eventually fall into place. Scheduling an argument lays the foundation for good communication. You're less likely to have a big fight or shut each other out.

ADMIT WHEN YOU ARE WRONG

People with ADD tend to vigorously defend themselves even after they realize they are wrong. Some people with ADD are inherently stubborn. Apologizing does not mean that you accept the other person's behavior or agree with her opinion. By apologizing, you are saying that you acted in a way that was not fair or considerate to the other person. If you feel you have slighted someone, say you are sorry. The words are simple, but the impact on your relationships is great.

Do not tell someone "I told you so," even if you know you are right. This upsets the other person and does not help either of you. Chances are the other person already knows you were right. Do not rub it in.

SEEK PROFESSIONAL HELP FOR YOUR ANGER

When you feel you have lost control over your anger, you have become increasingly angry, and/or your health and relationships have been affected, I recommend that you seek the assistance of a mental health professional. You can learn more about counseling services later in this chapter, and information about locating a therapist can be found at the end of this chapter.

Find a Compatible Partner

It can be difficult enough to find a compatible partner even without considering how ADD will affect your future relationship. Since people with ADD tend to become totally consumed with a relationship once it's under way, it is best to start with a clear idea of what you are looking for in a mate, including whether you would prefer a partner who does or does not have ADD. Defining what you want in a partner increases your chances of relationship success.

Take out a sheet of paper and write down everything you are looking for in a mate. Ideas include *gets along well with my family, likes to travel, is a good cook, or likes the outdoors.* You could even write down that your ideal mate must like your dog. The more specific, the better.

The next time you think you have met your special someone, review this list and see how well this person matches your criteria. Decide if the qualities that do not match are qualities you're willing to give up. It depends on how important those qualities are to you.

Enhance Your Sexual Intimacy with Your Partner

People with ADD are more prone to have affairs—and also, to the contrary, more likely to have low sex drive. Affairs may happen when a person with ADD quickly becomes bored with a relationship. Many people with ADD start relationships hot and heavy, getting involved with great intensity.

The sex life of a person with ADD presents an interesting dilemma. How do you have a sex life with variety, yet still stay faithful to your partner? You can remain monogamous and have variety; the two are not separate concepts. You can bring variety to your sex life using different sexual positions and different locations. Some people with ADD don't like being touched in the same place in the same way over and over. Try asking your partner to vary the type of touch.

Having a low sex drive means that you feel uninterested in sex—like it is not worth the trouble. Depression, which frequently goes along with ADD, can cause low sex drive. You may also have a low sex drive because you are not able to pay attention and focus during sex. It is vital to explain to your partner that your low sex drive is due to reasons other than the attractiveness of your partner. You also may not have been able to have an orgasm because you could not focus. Talk to your doctor if you have low sex drive or difficulty focusing. Medications, such as the ones you learned about in chapter 2, can help you regain your focus.

Long periods of sexual activity can leave you feeling overwhelmed or give you a feeling of sensory overload. You may need to participate in sexual activity for shorter periods of time so your focus does not wander. Better communication with your partner can improve your sex life.

PREVENT AN UNPLANNED PREGNANCY

Each year, many people with ADD face unplanned pregnancies. An unplanned pregnancy greatly adds to the stress of a relationship. Unplanned pregnancies can be more common in people with ADD for two reasons. First, if a woman with ADD is prescribed birth control pills, she may not remember to take the pill every night. Second, people with ADD are impulsive, and in the throes of passion, they may forget or even deliberately choose not to use a condom. This not only increases the risk of unplanned pregnancy, it also increases the risk of sexually transmitted diseases (STDs).

While condoms are the best way to prevent the transmission of STDs, you may want to use a low-maintenance form of contraception—one that does not need to be taken every day or used each time you have intercourse. Low-maintenance forms of birth control include the following methods, administered by health care professionals:

- The intrauterine device (IUD), which is inserted into the uterus and can last up to twelve years

- A hormonal implant, which is inserted into a woman's arm and can last up to three years

- A hormonal injection, which lasts three months

- Sterilization, such as a tubal ligation for women and a vasectomy for men, performed by a doctor (in most cases, sterilization is permanent and not reversible)

Seek Outside Help

You may find that you have tried improving your relationships or quality of life without noticing much progress. A neutral third party can help you and your partner solve relationship problems. There is help available when you feel your relationships are in a rut or have become destructive.

Counseling is a way to get help not only for yourself but also for your family. There are counselors who specialize in working with couples and families. When you first contact a counselor, ask if she has experience working with couples and families. Also ask if she has experience helping people with ADD. You can look up counselors who specialize in ADD at the websites listed at the end of this chapter.

Ask the counselor about the fee per session. You can also ask if the counselor accepts insurance or if you pay the fee in full and receive a receipt from the counselor that you can send to your insurance company for reimbursement. The amount of reimbursement (if any) depends on your insurance company. Be aware that if you file an insurance claim, the information—including your diagnosis—may affect your chances of getting health, life, or disability insurance in the future. You can find information about a medical-information clearinghouse at the end of this chapter.

In this chapter, you learned how to enhance your relationships and improve communication with your family and friends. Throughout this book, you have learned how having ADD affects your life and what you can do to improve your quality of life. The following exercise will help you gain insight as to how much you have learned since you started this book.

Exercise: Look at How Much You Have Learned

When you started reading this book, you most likely were looking for answers and tips about ADD and the challenges it presents. It is time to look back on the knowledge you have gained. You have learned about

- the symptoms of ADD

- myths and facts about ADD

- medications available for treating ADD

- strategies for improving your organizational skills

- ways to avoid losing your belongings

- improving money management

- maintaining wellness and balance in your life

- finding the career that is best for you

- improving your social skills

- enriching your relationships

Now answer the following questions:

- What was your perception of ADD when you first started the book?

- How has your perception changed?

- What changes have you seen in yourself since you started the book?

- What changes have you noticed in your family and friends since you started the book?

- What is the most important thing you have learned about having ADD?

- What areas do you need to work on?

- What goals would you like to reach one year from now?

- What goals would you like to reach five years from now?

- What is the most important thing you have learned about having ADD?

- What areas do you need to work on?

- What goals would you like to reach one year from now?

- What goals would you like to reach five years from now?

When you are having difficulties in a particular area of your life, refer back to this book and reread your list of goals so you can steer yourself down the right path. Remember that life is about your journey, not your destination.

Resources

Gottman, J., and N. Silver. 2000. *The Seven Principles for Making Marriage Work: A Practical Guide from the Country's Foremost Relationship Expert.* New York: Three Rivers Press.

Hallowell, E.H., S. Hallowell, and M. Orlov. 2010. *Married to Distraction: Restoring Intimacy and Strengthening Your Marriage in an Age of Interruption.* New York: Ballantine Books.

Pera, G. 2008. *Is It You, Me, or Adult A.D.D.?: Stopping the Roller Coaster When Someone You Love Has Attention Deficit Disorder.* San Francisco: 1201 Alarm Press.

ADD Referral
www.addreferral.com

American Counseling Association
www.counseling.org

Medical Information Bureau
www.mib.com
For MIB record information: (866) 692-6901

Psychology.com
www.psychology.com

The Family & Marriage Counseling Directory
www.family-marriage-counseling.com

TherapistLocator.net
The American Association for Marriage and Family
Therapy
www.therapistlocator.net

References

Altfas, J. R. 2002. Prevalence of attention-deficit/hyperactivity disorder among adults in obesity treatment. *BMC Psychiatry* 2(1): 9.

Anatalis, C. J., L. J. Stevens, M. Campbell, R. Pazdro, K. Ericson, and J. R. Burgess. 2006. Omega-3 fatty acid status in attention-deficit/hyperactivity disorder. *Prostaglandins, Leukotrienes and Essential Fatty Acids* 75(4–5): 299–308.

Barkley, R. A. 2005. *Attention-Deficit Hyperactivity Disorder: A Handbook for Diagnosis and Treatment.* 3rd ed. New York: The Guilford Press.

Barkley, R. A., M. Fischer, L. Smallish, and K. Fletcher. 2005. Young adult outcome of hyperactive children: Adaptive functioning in major life activities. *Journal of the American Academy of Child and Adolescent Psychiatry* 45(2): 192–202.

Barkley, R. A., M. Fischer, L. Smallish, and K. Fletcher. 2002. The persistence of attention-deficit/hyperactivity disorder into adulthood as a function of reporting source and definition of disorder. *Journal of Abnormal Psychology* 111: 279–89.

Barkley, R. A., and K. R. Murphy. 1998. *Attention-Deficit Hyperactivity Disorder: A Clinical Workbook.* New York: The Guilford Press.

Barkley, R. A., K. R. Murphy, and M. Fischer. 2008. *ADHD in Adults: What the Science Says*. New York: The Guilford Press.

Bernfort, L., S. Nordfeldt, and J. Persson. 2008. ADD from a socioeconomic perspective. *Acta Paediatrica* 97(2): 239–45.

Biederman J., R. D. Melmed, A. Patel, K. McBurnett, J. Konow, A. Lyne, and N. Scherer, for the SPD503 Study Group. 2008. A randomized, double-blind, placebo-controlled study of guanfacine extended release in children and adolescents with attention-deficit/hyperactivity disorder. *Pediatrics* 121(1): e73–e84.

Biederman, J., S. W. Ball, M. C. Monuteaux, C. B. Surman, J. L. Johnson, and S. Zeitlin. 2007. Are girls with ADHD at risk for eating disorders? Results from a controlled, five-year prospective study. *Journal of Developmental and Behavioral Pediatrics* 28(4): 302–7.

Breyer, J., A. Botzet, K. Winters, R. Stinchfield, and G. August. 2009. Young adult gambling behaviors and their relationship with the persistence of ADD. *Journal of Gambling Studies* 25(2): 227–38.

Brown, T. E. 2009. ADD/ADD and impaired executive function in clinical practice. *Current Attention Disorders Reports* 1(1): 37–41.

Brown, T. E. 1996. *Brown Attention-Deficit Disorder Scales*. San Antonio, TX: Psychological Corporation.

Brown, T. E., and J. M. Landgraf. 2010. Improvements in executive function correlate with enhanced performance and functioning and health-related quality of life: Evidence from 2 large, double-blind, randomized, placebo-controlled trials in ADHD. *Postgraduate Medicine* 122(5): 42–51.

Conners, C. K., D. Erhardt, and E. Sparrow. 1999. Conners' Adult ADD Rating Scales (CAARS). North Tonawanda, NY: Multi-Health Systems, Inc.

Consumers Union of the United States. Extended warranties: Say yes, sometimes. 2005. *Consumer Reports*, January.

Davis, C., R. D. Levitan, M. Smith, S. Tweed, and C. Curtis. 2006. Associations among overeating, overweight, and attention deficit/hyperactivity disorder: A structural equation modelling approach. *Eating Behaviors* 7(3): 266–74.

DuPaul, G. J., T. J. Power, A. D. Anastopoulos, and R. Reid. 1998. *ADD Rating Scale—IV: Checklists, Norms, and Clinical Interpretation.* New York: The Guilford Press.

Elia, J., X. Gai, H. M. Xie, J.C. Perin, E. Geiger, J. T. Glessner, M. D'arcy, R. deBerardinis, E. Frackelton, C. Kim, F. Lantieri, B. M. Muganga, L. Wang, T. Takeda, E. F. Rappaport, S.F. Grant, W. Berrettini, M. Devoto, T.H. Shaikh, H. Hakonarson, P.S. White. 2010. Rare structural variants found in attention-deficit hyperactivity disorder are preferentially associated with neurodevelopmental genes. Molecular Psychiatry 15: 637–46.

Flory, K., B. S. Molina, W. E. Pelham, E. Gnagy, and B. Smith. 2006. Childhood ADD predicts risky sexual behavior in young adulthood. *Journal of Clinical Child and Adolescent Psychology* 35(4): 571–77.

Grow, B. 2005. The great rebate runaround. *Bloomberg Businessweek,* November 23. www.businessweek.com/bwdaily/dnflash/nov2005/nf20051123_4158_db016.htm.

Gruber, R., T. Xi, S. Frenette, M. Robert, P. Vannasinh, and J. Carrier. 2008. Sleep disturbances in prepubertal children with attention deficit hyperactivity disorder: A home polysomnography study. *Sleep* 32(3): 343–50.

Guan, L., B. Wang, Y. Chen, L. Yang, J. Li, and Q. Qian. 2009. A high-density single-nucleotide polymorphism screen of 23 candidate genes in attention deficit hyperactivity disorder: Suggesting multiple susceptibility genes among Chinese Han population. *Molecular Psychiatry* 14(5): 546–54.

Halmey, A., O. B. Fasmer, C. Gillberg, and J. Haavik. 2009. Occupational outcome in adult ADD: Impact of symptom profile, comorbid psychiatric problems, and treatment. *Journal of Attention Disorders* 13(2): 175–87.

Hammerness, P., R. Doyle, M. Kotarski, A. Georgiopoulos, G. Joshi, S. Zeitlin, and J. Biederman. 2009. Atomoxetine in children with attention-deficit hyperactivity disorder with prior stimulant therapy: A prospective open-label study. *European Child & Adolescent Psychiatry* 18(8): 493–98.

Huesmann, L. R., and L. D. Taylor. 2006. The role of media violence in violent behavior. *Annual Review of Public Health* 27: 393–415.

Kaufman-Scarborough, C., and J. Cohen. 2004. Unfolding consumer impulsivity: An existential-phenomenological study of consumers with attention deficit disorder. Psychology and Marketing 21 (8): 637–69.

Kessler R. C., L. Adler, M. Ames, O. Demler, S. Faraone, E. Hiripi, M. J. Howes, R. Jin, K. Secnik, T. Spencer, T. B. Ustun, and E. E. Walters. 2005. The World Health Organization adult ADHD self-report scale (ASRS): A short screening scale for use in the general population. *Psychological Medicine* 35(2): 245–56.

Kiluk, B. D., S. Weden, and V. Culotta. 2009. Sport participation and anxiety in children with ADHD. *Journal of Attention Disorders* 12(6): 499–506.

Kleinman, N. L., M. Durkin, A. Melkonian, and K. Markosyan. 2009. Incremental employee health benefit costs, absence days, and turnover among employees with ADD and among employees with children with ADD. *Journal of Occupational and Environmental Medicine* 51(11): 1247–55.

Lindsay, S. E., G. A. Gudelsky, and P. C. Heaton. 2006. Use of modafinil for the treatment of attention deficit/hyperactivity disorder. *Annals of Pharmacotherapy* 40(10): 1829–33.

Mannuzza S., R. G. Klein, N. L. Truong, J. L. Moulton, III, E. R. Roizen, K. H. Howell, and F. X. Castellanos. 2008. Age of methylphenidate treatment initiation in children with ADHD and later substance abuse: Prospective follow-up into adulthood. *American Journal of Psychiatry* 165(5): 604–9.

Mathews, V. P., W. G. Kronenberger, Y. Wang, J. T. Lurito, M. J. Lowe, and D. Dunn. 2005. Media violence exposure and frontal lobe activation measured by functional magnetic resonance imaging in aggressive and nonaggressive adolescents. *Journal of Computer Assisted Tomography* 29(3): 287–92.

Mazaheri, A., S. Coffey-Corina, G. R. Mangun, E. M. Bekker, A. S. Berry, and B. A. Corbett. 2010. Functional disconnection of frontal cortex and visual cortex in attention-deficit/hyperactivity disorder. *Biological Psychiatry* 67(7): 617–23.

McAlonan G. M., V. Cheung, S. E. Chua, J. Oosterlaan, S. F. Hung, C. P. Tang, C. C. Lee, S. L. Kwong, T. P. Ho, C. Cheung, J. Suckling, and P. W. Leung. 2009. Age-related grey matter volume correlates of response inhibition and shifting in attention-deficit hyperactivity disorder. *British Journal of Psychiatry* 194(2): 123–9.

Michelson, D., L. Adler, T. Spencer, F. W. Reimherr, S. A. West, A. J. Allen, D. Kelsey, J. Wernicke, A. Dietrich, and D. Milton. 2003. Atomoxetine in adults with ADHD: Two randomized placebo-controlled studies. *Biological Psychiatry* 53(2): 112–20.

Milian, M. 2010. Reading on iPad before bed can affect sleep habits. *Los Angeles Times*, April 24. http: //latimesblogs.latimes.com/technology/2010/04/ipad-kindle-ebook-sleep.html.

Newcorn, J. H., C. J. Kratochvil, A. J. Allen, C. D. Casat, D. D. Ruff, R. J. Moore, D. Michelson, and Atomoxetine/Methylphenidate Comparative Study Group. 2008. Atomoxetine and osmotically released methylphenidate for the treatment of attention deficit hyperactivity disorder: Acute comparison and differential response. *American Journal of Psychiatry* 165(6): 721–30.

Null, J. 2011. *Hyperthermia deaths of children in vehicles*. San Francisco: San Francisco State University, Department of Geosciences. Retrieved June 6, 2011 from http: //ggweather.com/heat/.

Orman, S. 1997. *The Nine Steps to Financial Freedom: Practical and Spiritual Steps So You Can Stop Worrying*. New York: Crown Publishers.

Quinlan, D. M. 2000. Assessment of attention-deficit/hyperactivity disorder and comorbidities. In *Attention Deficit Disorders and Comorbidities in Children, Adolescents, and Adults*, edited by T. E. Brown. Washington, DC: American Psychiatric Association.

Rietveld, M. J. H., J. J. Hudziak, M. Bartels, C. E. M. Beijsterveldt, and D. I. Boomsma. 2004. Heritability of attention problems in children: Longitudinal results from a study of twins, age 3 to 12. *Journal of Child Psychology and Psychiatry* 45(3): 577–88.

Sabuncuoglu, O. 2007. Traumatic dental injuries and attention-deficit/hyperactivity disorder: Is there a link? *Dental Traumatology* 23(3): 137–42.

Sanford, J. A., and A. Turner. 2004. *IVA+Plus™: Integrated Visual and Auditory Continuous Performance Test (IVA+Plus) Administration Manual*. Richmond, VA: BrainTrain Inc.

Sawni A. **2008**. Attention-deficit/hyperactivity disorder and complementary/alternative medicine. *Adolescent Medicine State of the Art Reviews* 19(2): 313–26, xi.

Schlenger, W. E., J. M. Caddell, L. Ebert, B. K. Jordan, K. M. Rourke, D. Wilson, L. Thalji, J. M. Dennis, J. A. Fairbank, and R. A. Kulka. 2002. Psychological reactions to terrorist attacks: Findings from the National Study of Americans' Reactions to September 11. *Journal of.the American Medical Association* 288 (5): 581–88.

Schuchardt, J. P., M. Huss, M. Stauss-Grabo, and A. Hahn. 2010. Significance of long-chain polyunsaturated fatty acids (PUFAs) for the development and behaviour of children. *European Journal of Pediatrics* 169(2): 149–64.

Schredl, M., B. Alm, and E. Sobanski. 2007. Sleep quality in adult patients with attention deficit hyperactivity disorder (ADHD). *Journal of Attention Disorders* 10(3): 257–60.

Secnik, K., A. Swensen, and M. J. Lage. 2005. Comorbidities and costs of adult patients diagnosed with attention-deficit/hyperactivity disorder. *Pharmacoeconomics* 23(1): 93–102.

Silk, T. G. 2004. Examining purchase and non-redemption of mail-in rebates: The impact of offer variables on consumers' subjective and objective probability of redeeming. http: //etd.fcla.edu/UF/UFE0004380/silk_t.pdf

Sinn, N., and J. Bryan. 2007. Effect of supplementation with polyunsaturated fatty acids and micronutrients on learning and behavior problems associated with child ADHD. *Journal of Developmental and Behavioral Pediatrics* 28(2): 82–91.

Smith, S. L., A. I. Nathanson, and B. J. Wilson. 2002. Prime-time television: Assessing violence during the most popular viewing hours. *Journal of Communication* 52(1) 84–111.

Soat, J. 2007. Thoughts on dealing with identity theft. *InformationWeek*, March 12.

Solhkhah, R., T. E. Wilens, J. Daly, J. B. Prince, S. L. Van Patten, and J. Biederman. 2005. Bupropion SR for the treatment of substance-abusing outpatient adolescents with attention-deficit/hyperactivity disorder and mood disorders. *Journal of Child and Adolescent Psychopharmacology* 15(5): 777–86.

Spencer, T. J., J. M. Landgraf, L. A. Adler, R. H. Weisler, C. S. Anderson, and S. H. Youcha. 2008. Attention-deficit/hyperactivity disorder-specific quality of life with triple-bead mixed amphetamine salts (SPD465) in adults: Results of a randomized, double-blind, placebo-controlled study. *The Journal of Clinical Psychiatry* 69(11): 1766–75.

Thompson, A. L., B. S. Molina, W. Pelham, and E. M. Gnagy. 2007. Risky driving in adolescents and young adults with childhood ADD. *Journal of Pediatric Psychology* 32(7): 745–59.

Transler, C., A. Eilander, S. Mitchell, and N. van de Meer. 2010. The impact of polyunsaturated fatty acids in reducing child attention deficit and hyperactivity disorders. *Journal of Attention Disorders* 14(3): 232–46.

Triolo, S. J., and K. R. Murphy. 1996. Attention Deficit Scales for Adults (ADSA) Manual for Scoring and Interpretation. New York: Brunner/Mazel.

Uekermann, J., M. Kraemer, M. Abdel-Hamid, B. G. Schimmelmann, J. Hebebrand, I. Daum, J. Wiltfang, and B. Kis. 2010. Social cognition in attention-deficit hyperactivity disorder (ADHD). *Neuroscience & Biobehavioral Reviews* 34(5): 734–43.

Van Veen, M. M., J. J. S. Kooij, A. N. Boonstra, M. C. M. Gordijn, and E. J. W. van Someren. 2010. Delayed circadian rhythm in adults with attention-deficit/hyperactivity disorder and chronic sleep-onset insomnia. *Biological Psychiatry* 67(11): 1091–96.

Vaughan B., J. Fegert, and C. J. Kratochvil. 2009. Update on atomoxetine in the treatment of attention-deficit/hyperactivity disorder. *Expert Opinion on Pharmacotherapy* 10(4): 669–76.

Volkow N. D., G. J. Wang, S. H. Kollins, T. L. Wigal, J. H. Newcorn, F. Telang, J. S. Fowler, W. Zhu, J. Logan, Y. Ma, K. Pradhan, C. Wong, and J. M. Swanson. 2009. Evaluating dopamine reward pathway in ADHD: Clinical implications. *Journal of the American Medical Association* 302(10): 1084–91.

Wagner, M. L., A. S. Walters, and B. C. Fisher. 2004. Symptoms of attention-deficit/hyperactivity disorder in adults with restless leg syndrome. *Sleep* 27(8): 1499–1504.

Walters, A. S., R. Silvestri, M. Zucconi, R. Chandrashekariah, and E. Konofal. 2008. Review of the possible relationship and hypothetical links between attention deficit hyperactivity disorder (ADHD) and the simple sleep related movement disorders, parasomnias, hypersomnias, and circadian rhythm disorders. *Journal of Clinical Sleep Medicine* 4(6): 591–600.

Ward, M. F., P. H. Wender, and F. W. Reimherr. 1993. The Wender Utah Rating Scale: An aid in the retrospective diagnosis of childhood attention deficit hyperactivity disorder. *American Journal of Psychiatry* 150(8): 885–90.

Weiss, M., L. T. Hechtman, and G. Weiss. 1999. *ADD in Adulthood: A Guide to Current Theory, Diagnosis, and Treatment*. Baltimore: The Johns Hopkins University Press.

Wigal, S. B. 2009. Efficacy and safety limitations of attention-deficit hyperactivity disorder pharmacotherapy in children and adults. *CNS Drugs* 23(Suppl. 1): 21–31.

Wilens, T. E. 2004. Attention-deficit/hyperactivity disorder and the substance use disorders: The nature of the relationship, subtypes at risk, and treatment issues. *Psychiatric Clinics of North America* 27(2): 283–301.

Wilens, T. E., S. V. Faraone, J. Biederman, and S. Gunawardene. 2003. Does stimulant therapy of attention-deficit/hyperactivity disorder beget later substance abuse? A meta-analytic review of the literature. *Pediatrics* 111: 179–85.

Wilens, T. E., and H. P. Upadhyaya. 2007. Impact of substance use disorder on ADHD and its treatment. *Journal of Clinical Psychiatry* 68(8): e20.

Wolf, J. R., H. R. Arkes, and W. A. Muhanna. 2008. The power of touch: An examination of the effect of duration of physical contact on the valuation of objects. *Judgment and Decision Making* 3(6): 476–82.

Young, G. S., J. A. Conquer, and R. Thomas. 2005. Effect of supplementation with polyunsaturated fatty acids and micronutrients on learning and behavior problems associated with child ADHD. *Reproduction, Nutrition, Development* 45(5): 549–58.

Stephanie Moulton Sarkis, PhD, is an adjunct assistant professor at Florida Atlantic University in Boca Raton, FL, and author of *Making the Grade with ADD*, *ADD and Your Money*, and *Adult ADD: A Guide for the Newly Diagnosed*. She is a licensed mental health counselor and national certified counselor, and has a private counseling practice. Sarkis won an American Psychological Association Outstanding Dissertation Award in 2001. She has been published in the *Journal of Attention Disorders and Smart Money Magazine*, and writes for *Psychology Today* and *The Huffington Post*. She has made several national and regional media appearances on CNN, ABC, Fox, Sirius Satellite Radio, First Business, and other media outlets. Visit her online at www.stephaniesarkis.com.